The results have been amazing! I nc  *focus and determination. If you're* *your career and life to the next level th* *ork with Deborah Dubree.*

> — DJ Krust (aka K Thompson) co-owner of Full Cycle record label and The Disruptive Patterns Strategy Session Workshops, London, UK

Deborah is an expert... a technique person with the mind. She's the best I've run into! She has done an outstanding job presenting at my Free Agent Combines and Pro Development Camps for NFL hopefuls.

> — Coach Gary Zauner, 13 Years NFL Special Teams Coordinator, Owner-Coach Zauner, LLC

Deborah's workshops always receive great reviews. She does an outstanding job of presenting interesting and real world actionable content, as she fully engages the participants.

> — Carolyn Boettner, National Administrator, Timberline Users Group, Inc.

Deborah Dubree's sessions with my clients have been invaluable in achieving optimal performance at critical events leading up to the NFL draft. All achieved significantly better than anticipated results! Her methods gave them the confidence and tools required to maximize their talents.

> — Jerry Marlatt: President of First Team Sports Group

Deborah Dubree is a tell-it-like-it-is speaker with an ability to make you realize that even your best can get better. She is warm and engaging while setting the record straight. One minute you are laughing and the next minute you are taking notes. She is a wow.

> — Inc. 500 Honoree

FROM **MEDIOCRE** TO **MILLIONS!**

AVERAGE IS AN ADDICTION

Russ !
Up Yours !
Up Your Power,
Up Your Performance
Up Your Position
Wish You the Best !

Deborah

FROM MEDIOCRE TO MILLIONS!

From Receptionist to CEO of a
$20 Million Construction Company ...
with Only a High School Diploma

DEBORAH DUBREE

Published by

ClearEDGE, LLC
Phoenix, Arizona

Copyright © 2013 by ClearEdge, LLC and Deborah M. Dubree.

All rights reserved, including the right to reproduce this book or portions thereof in any form whatsoever.

No part of this publication may be reproduced, distributed or transmitted in any form or by any means, including photocopying, recording, or other electronic or mechanical methods, without the prior written permission of the publisher, except in the case of brief quotations embodied in critical reviews and certain other noncommercial uses permitted by copyright law.

For permission requests, write to the publisher, addressed: Attention: Permissions Coordinator at: info@DeborahDubree.com

Ordering Information: Quantity sales.
Special discounts are available on quantity purchases by corporations, associations, and others. For details, contact the "Special Sales Department" at info@DeborahDubree.com.

Average Is An Addiction / Deborah Dubree -1st ed.
ISBN 978-0-9823646-7-3

This book is dedicated
to my two beautiful, talented, intelligent,
courageous and creative children

Kristine and Jason.

Thank you for being you …
and for always supporting and encouraging
me to be me!

Love & Hugs,
Mom

CONTENTS

CONTENTS

INTRODUCTION

Why am I writing this book? I think being average is for sissies. Staying stuck in average is stupid.

I see it all the time; don't you? People quit right before they get what they say they want most. They stop short of doing what it takes to win big and win often. They back down when a challenge feels too big or they think the challenge is greater than their current capabilities. Why be average?

I've never been able to figure it out. Who would ever want to be average? No one pays attention to, or gives a crap about, average. Average means you get lumped in with everybody else who is average.

People who stay average are not recognized or respected. They will never earn the big bucks or achieve what they ultimately want in life. They settle.

Everybody is different. Our wants are different. For some, what they want most is their dream job. For others, it's a championship ring, a million dollar income or to be an extraordinary leader. Yet others want to finally get paid what they know they are worth, rather than a cheap dollars-for-hours rate of pay. So, what happens? Why do people settle?

They will talk about what they want, plan for it, and yearn for it. They firmly state over and over again that they would do anything to get what they want. But they won't.

Instead, when they hit the wall of overwhelm, fear, frustration, anxiety and stress they give up. They continually undermine their own success. At the very moment when they should be pushing the limits of their capabilities, they push the panic button. They give in and settle in to being average.

They Have Become Addicted to Average!

Keep in mind I'm talking about skilled, educated and talented people. These are people who have worked to develop their knowledge, talent and skillset. They have reached a level of success that provides them satisfaction ... up to a point.

Average feels safe. Average is for sissies.

– Deborah Dubree

How do I know that capable, educated, talented people are underperforming and getting stuck in average? How do I know that smart, caring, hardworking people are settling for less, instead of pushing the limits to be more, have more and enjoy more? Look around.

Have you ever attended a conference full of entrepreneurs? The room is filled with once top performers from the corporate world. They are the ones who used to shake things up. They were envied and admired. They achieved what others couldn't. Now they have moved on. They want more. Need to achieve more.

No longer having traditional nine-to-five jobs, these savvy entrepreneurs have entered a whole new career field. They want to educate themselves fast and go right to the top. It's time to once again become the movers and shakers among their peers.

So they gather at conferences to listen and learn from the so-called *"experts."* They are told what to do, how to do it and when to do it. They buy into the dream that they will become the next six-figure success story.

You can hear the rah-rah speeches and the, "You can do it!" battle cries ringing throughout the ballrooms and individual breakout sessions. Opportunities to learn are everywhere.

Entrepreneurs scramble around taking notes, making connections and sharing their action plans. Everything is in alignment. It all seems perfect. And then they go home.

Suddenly, the excitement is gone. Reality slaps them in the face. They become overwhelmed with thoughts of, "What am I supposed to do next? Why does everybody else get it and I don't?" Their disjointed thoughts begin to undermine any chance of real success.

The "Can Do" attitude is quickly replaced with unfamiliar feelings of overwhelm, doubt, fear and frustration. Feeling lost, forgotten and alone, they panic.

At the very moment these once high achievers should be making bold decisions and taking ballsy actions to get what they want, they remain confused and dazed.

They head off to the next teleseminar or conference, looking for someone else to solve their problems for them. Groping for the next so-called expert to tell them what to do. The cycle starts all over again. It's back to the drawing board. Back to average.

Got it? Sound familiar? Here's another example.

In business, millions of dollars are lost every single day because management and employees are ho-humming it through the workday. Drive, ambition, discipline and focus have become dirty words in the work force. Excelling above and beyond a job description is unheard of.

My skin crawls when I hear employees say, "I'm doing the

best I can!" That's code for, "This is as good as it's ever going to get. Live with it!!"

Just as pathetic is hearing people in authority, like business managers, coaches, parents or the so-called experts spout off, "Just do the best you can."

It makes me want to scream, REALLY! I mean it, really? Is that all we have come to expect?

It's sad. I always wait and watch to see if there will be a demeaning little pat on the head to follow the directions for low expectations.

When someone is "doing the best they can," it's a sign of weakness, not really giving a crap and barely putting in any effort. There is an expectation of failure that goes along with the statement.

Think about it this way: When you are building a loving relationship, how would you like to hear these words come out of the other person's mouth, "Honey, I'm doing the best I can!" Not exactly the most comforting words.

At that point, it's time for a choice. Either you can plan on settling for less than the other person's best or you can plan your exit strategy.

How about your customers or clients? Think about it. If a client had a problem with one of your products or with the delivery of one of your services and the client heard, "Well, I did the best I could," how long do you think that client would stick around?

That kind of attitude at any level or in any department has a direct hit on the bottom line of a company. It's time to hit the performance button ... before it becomes time to hit the panic button.

Here's my final example: I coach and train very successful top performers, both in business and in sports. At times, they become confused and concerned when all of a sudden their performance begins to level off. They plateau.

They begin to blend in and fit in. They start to settle for less. Less from themselves and less from others around them.

They are not happy with this feeling or the results of being 'good enough.' They are no longer a top performer when compared to their top-performing peers. Good enough is not who they are. But it is who they have become.

It's painful for a high achiever. It scares the hell out of them. They were once the envy of their peers and now they see themselves settling into average. They feel like they've lost their mojo and don't know how to get it back.

THIS IS IMPORTANT

Being smart, gifted, educated, knowledgeable, talented and skilled is not enough. There are thousands of people in your position and your industry who fit that description. It won't get you to the top and keep you there. It won't get you what you really want.

**Truly successful people
develop a competitive edge.**

~

**They make bold decisions.
They take bold and ballsy action.**

High achieving, successful people go after what they want. They don't expect it to come to them. If they don't like the hand they are dealt, rather than moaning and groaning about it, they will figure out a way to make it into a winning hand.

They do what it takes. When they hit the wall—and we all do—they bounce back quickly. They take control. Getting back on track fast is imperative to their success, and they know it.

Top Performers Outsmart the Obvious.
They don't accept things as they are.
They see things how they can be.

The choices and decisions of a top performer are not always obvious, or accepted or approved by others. But they don't give a crap. They do what's right for them. Their battle cry is, "I Got This!"

They do what's necessary. They do it fast. They do it without complaining. They act with an expectation of succeeding. They get what they want.

THIS BOOK IS NOT ABOUT ME

This is not a book of my memoirs. You will not learn about my passion and my purpose. I'm not going to be sharing my favorite foods or vacation spot.

However, to make specific points, and when it makes sense, I will share some of my personal and professional stories of struggle and success.

You will also read some carefully selected stories and examples from my clients, with their names changed. They represent an array of business professionals, sales experts, entrepreneurs, NFL players and pro golfers.

IS THIS BOOK FOR YOU?

This book is for you if you are competitive and committed to achieving more than you ever have before.

This is a must-read for business leaders, sales professionals, managers and your teams. It is critical for entrepreneurs, speakers and teachers.

It's for people who are sick and tired of making excuses for why they haven't reached the next level of their success. For people who are no longer willing to settle for second best and are serious about making a change now!

This book is for you if you are willing to be challenged, pushed and prodded to bring out your ultimate game:

- Maybe you want to develop an edge so you can outsmart your competition and get more of what you want.

- Maybe you're tired of seeing people with less knowledge, talent and intelligence get ahead, while you watch and wonder why this keeps happening.

- Maybe you are already successful, but know deep down there is more you want to accomplish. More you can achieve. You need someone powerful to give you a swift kick in the butt.

- Maybe you want to show up at the next family gathering and when your smart-mouthed brother-in-law asks, "What have you been up to?" you smile and share your latest accomplishments. His jaw-dropping look of envy is priceless.

- Or maybe you are tired of playing it safe. The thought of pushing the limits and challenging yourself to succeed beyond your own expectations of success is exhilarating. It's time!

THIS BOOK IS NOT FOR YOU

This book is not for people who are perfectly comfortable and happy with their life, career, position and finances exactly as they are now. If someone is unwilling to make a change, this is not the right book.

For people who are not competitive enough or committed enough to take charge of their life and push the limits of their capabilities, this book is not a good fit.

If wasting time, money and energy has become a favorite habit that you are just not willing to give up, this is not your kind of book.

Maybe the thought of digging deep and taking personal responsibility is too scary or too much to deal with right now.

Or, you kinda, maybe, almost want to make a change, but not enough to actually do something about it. No worries—this is not a good fit.

> *Everybody is waiting for you to fail . . .*
> *what are you waiting for?*

– Deborah Dubree

WHAT YOU CAN EXPECT FROM THIS BOOK

In this book, I'm going to share many specific examples of how you can capitalize, monetize and leverage your skills, intelligence, talents and competitive attitude. You will be surprised at what opportunities you've been missing.

I will share specific steps for becoming more bold and ballsy, so you get more of what you want. Learn how to gain a competitive edge over your competition. Replace hesitation and procrastination with the courage to take action.

When you focus on performing at your ultimate and competitive best, make bold decisions and take the appropriate ballsy action, you will achieve far more than even you believe you are capable of achieving. I can prove it!

Average must be avoided. I will share exactly what will trip you up and take you down if you're not paying attention to the warning signs.

I'm going to share my insights and strategies that I use when successfully coaching and training my business professionals, sales experts, leaders, entrepreneurs, NFL players and pro golfers. They have learned to up their game, their income and their recognition.

I will reveal the various strategies that I have used to catapult my position, my paycheck and my power to influence and impact others.

WHAT YOU CAN'T EXPECT FROM THIS BOOK

Here's the thing: this book is not about telling someone how great he or she is. It's not about soothingly saying that everything will be okay if you simply apply yourself a bit more. That kind of wishy-washy nonsense would be a waste of time, effort and money.

This is not a book debating why women or men should or should not be ambitious. I like ambition. It has served me well.

This is not about time management, how to organize your

office or balance your life. This is not a "let's hold hands and sing, 'We Are The World'" book.

I am not going to address people who have no desire to make a change or who want to argue with what has repeatedly been proven to work successfully.

I'm not trying to win you over to my side. People who take action win. Those who don't, lose. You make the choice!

WHY ME? WHY NOW?

I went from receptionist to owner and CEO of a $20 million commercial construction company, with only a high school diploma. I am bold and ballsy, and I back that up with taking the right actions.

I am a living, breathing example of what can happen when people do not allow circumstances, education, society, hardships or economics define who they are or who they can become. Here's how it happened for me:

After selling my company, I wanted to share what I had learned, systematized and successfully implemented to catapult my own career. These are the same training and coaching methods I now offer my highly competitive, ambitious, talented and committed business professionals and athletes.

I enjoy challenging my clients. They all want to perform at their ultimate best. They all want to get noticed, make a lot more money and earn the respect they deserve. Developing a clear and competitive edge is important to them. And they all want to learn from someone who has done it.

Nothing is ever smooth or easy. Anyone who tells you that being highly successful is a smooth ride is lying. But the struggles are worth it.

For myself, being successful meant being a single mom of two children, juggling a career, my kids, kids' sports, school conferences, business travels and three dogs. Plus balancing finances, bandaging various body parts and all the rest that goes with being a loving and supportive parent.

Let's add in coping with divorce, bankruptcy, the death of both of my parents plus two business partners, the suicide of a valued employee and my own surgeries and illnesses.

On the upside, my success has provided me the opportunity to feed my love for travel. I have enjoyed visiting several African countries, as well as London, Australia and New Zealand.

Satisfying my need for speed and adventure has been fulfilled through snorkeling the Great Barrier Reef, cage diving with great white sharks, whale watching from a raft, enjoying tented safaris and driving a 600-horsepower NASCAR racecar at 124 mph.

For over thirty-seven years, I studied, developed and applied the most advanced positive psychology, cutting-edge stress reduction methods, neuroscience, neuro-linguistic programming (NLP) and hypnosis to myself. I now share simple, powerful, effective and easy-to-apply systems and techniques with my clients.

My Reward: I have earned the right and the freedom to make my own choices.

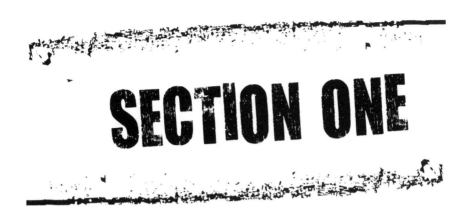

SECTION ONE

ACCEPTING AVERAGE
IS ACCEPTING FAILURE

Accepting average is accepting failure. It is a form of giving up and giving in. It's failing your Self. It is accepting that you cannot be any better than or achieve any more than where you currently are right now.

I do not believe in accepting circumstances, education, society, hardships or economics as a definition of who you currently are or who you can become. You're better than that.

But far too often, people become comfortable doing the same thing over and over again. I'll bet you drive the same route to work every day. Eat the same type of foods from the same places. Watch the same type of television shows, read the same type of books and visit the same type of social networking sites. It's predictable and it feels safe. You are predictable.

YOU ARE AN ADDICT TO YOUR OWN BEHAVIORS

People also repeat the same old patterns in their career and in their performance. They do the same type of work, in the same familiar way, with the same type of people, in the same or similar surroundings.

They will complain about what they have always complained about. The only difference will be a change in some of the names, the faces and their circumstances.

Becoming addicted to average is simple. In fact, it's a formula.

Average thoughts equals average behaviors.

Average behaviors lead to average results.

Average results are followed by average consequences.

And you live with the consequences!

It doesn't have to be that way. There are options. But until the addiction to average is broken and replaced with excellence, the addictive pattern of average will continue.

That is why I've written Section One. I want to ensure that you are clear, crystal clear, about what is at stake. Then, you can make an informed decision to stay stuck in average or move into excellence!

CHAPTER ONE

Average Sucks
And I Can Prove It

In my experience, very few people have the guts, determination, discipline and commitment to break out of average and become the greatest at what they do.

Some people don't want to change. Others have settled into being moderately satisfied with their current level of success. Still others didn't even realize they had options.

I'm not even going to address the first group. They're hopeless. The other two groups—I've got lots to share with you!

I don't know about you, but I see it all the time. People "touch and run." They will touch excellence and then run back to average. They become too scared or too overwhelmed to stay in excellence. They second-guess themselves. Doubt creeps in, and they question if they are really good enough to stay excellent. Average is their safety net.

So before jumping into sharing what it takes to truly perform at a high level, it's important to take a hard look at average. What is average? How can the sissy behaviors of average be avoided?

What are the consequences of getting stuck in average? Why should you care? What's really at stake? Are you willing to pay the heavy price of staying stuck in average?

I'll cover all of these questions throughout the chapters in Section One. These questions are too important to ignore or glance over. I want to ensure that you will be successful at breaking the addiction to average and then take the action necessary to move into excellence.

AVERAGE SUCKS

Average sucks motivation, intelligence and talent right out of highly competitive people. It sucks up opportunities for advancement and blinds them to opportunities for growth.

Being average is a choice. Moment to moment, there are opportunities to be bold, take charge and push the limits of performance. It's up to each individual to decide to take action.

Pain is a great motivator for breaking out of average. When people experience enough pain, they are faced with a choice. Push the panic button or push themselves into action.

SUCK IT UP

The multimillion-dollar contract and various bonuses were a big freakin' deal to Travis. So was being drafted into the NFL. His path to success had been a struggle.

As the son of a proud single mom from Alabama, he was now "the man." His hopes and dreams were fulfilled. He had beat the statistics. Only 2.4% of college football players make it into the NFL each year. Travis was one of the chosen.

But after eight years as a starter on the defensive line, his body was sore. It had begun to slow down from all of the bone-crushing hits. The weekly swirling ice baths to numb the pain and reduce his swelling muscles had become a grind.

Every week during his eight seasons, he pushed his mind and body to the limit. He left it all out on the field every single game. But the painful reality was starting to hit him hard.

Travis began to see the signs. With his thirtieth birthday approaching, he was quickly becoming one of the old guys in the league. Young blood was coming up through the draft, and they were eager and hungry to take his position away from him.

Fear began ripping at his gut. Travis's heart wasn't in the game anymore. His fierce determination had been replaced with worry and frustration. The very thought of sitting on the bench during a game and watching some other player start in his position sickened him.

He knew that his value to the team would drop. If Travis lost the starting position, he would also lose big money. Really big money. A new contract might only be for a year or two. And it would be for substantially less money.

His feelings of disappointment and disgust were worse than any bone-crushing hits he had endured. Travis was on the brink of being reduced to "just one of the guys." This was not acceptable.

Travis could feel his dream slipping away. Giving up on himself and on his dream was scary as hell. After a few weeks of wallowing in self-pity, Travis finally took his hand off the panic button.

Average was not in his nature. Quitting wasn't, either. He decided to get off his ass, make a bold decision and take some ballsy action.

In less than a week of our working together, Travis went back to being disciplined in his workouts and his training. He began to regain the confidence and cockiness he had as a rookie. He was fighting hard to remain at that starting position.

Travis went back to pushing his mind and his body to even greater levels of strength, endurance and performance.

Commitment to excellence paid off. Travis remained focused on his job. His job was to play hard, not just in every game, but also on every single play. Once again, he believed in himself and his talent.

He beat the crap out of average! He signed a five-year contract and earned the right to remain the starter. But it took experiencing immense pain to push Travis into taking ballsy action.

Do nothing and nothing changes. You're stuck.

Everyone runs the risk of being sucked into average—even if they were once ambitious, competitive, hungry for new challenges and looked for opportunities to achieve greatness.

It doesn't matter how smart they are, how talented they might be, how much skill they have or the level of their education. Average can and will suck anyone in.

An executive who sits in a high-backed leather chair in a corner office and wears Armani suits can get sucked into average. Average can suck in a receptionist juggling phones at the front desk.

Think about average this way: if you look, act, smell, sound, feel and behave like everyone else in your peer group, you are average. If you are not going above and beyond "the standard," you're average. Boom!

MAKING THE CUT

During our drive, Jeff, an NFL scout, and I were sharing our war stories and battle scars from working in the field of professional football.

Bad weather caused us both to miss our connecting flights into Mobile, Alabama. We decided it was quicker to share a rental car and drive to our destination than to book another flight.

Mobile, Alabama, is the site of the annual prestigious Senior Bowl. This is where top college football prospects from around the country are invited to showcase their talents, in hopes of becoming the next multimillion-dollar superstar to be drafted into the NFL.

NFL team coaches, scouts and trainers grade and scrutinize every single player on their performance both on and off the playing field. Each year, millions of contract dollars are at stake.

Players are measured, weighed, poked, prodded and interviewed. Every day during field practice, along with the ultimate finale All-Star Game, the NFL teams look for cracks in the armor of these kids. They want to know which players have what it takes to make it into the NFL and stay there.

For the players, this is the time to go big or go home. Everything they have worked for since Pop Warner football is on the line.

I was attending to connect with potential clients. The NFL scouts, coaches and trainers were attending to find the next breakout players.

Our long drive into Mobile provided a rare opportunity. Jeff was captured in the car and I had questions. I wanted to get his perspective.

So I asked Jeff how he goes about grading this talented pool of players. What starts to separate those who will make it from those who won't be worth an NFL team's investment of time and money? What he said next pretty much sums up average:

> *"When I recommend players to my team, I've got to get it right. My job and millions of dollars are at stake. The first thing I do is see who's got the 'it' factor.*
>
> *Being talented and being skilled at their individual positions isn't enough. These guys are all talented, or they wouldn't be here.*
>
> *Someone has to stand out. He has to show me that he can handle the immense pressure of this situation and still perform. When he screws up, he'd better recover fast and get his head back in the game and on to the next play.*
>
> *The first thing I do is separate the ones with the 'it' factor. I can guarantee you there will only be a couple of these guys. I know they at least have a chance of being successful in the league.*
>
> *Then I spot the guys at the bottom. Each year, there are always a few players who really shouldn't even be here. I don't waste my time looking at them.*
>
> *Then there are all the other guys. The majority of the players. The ones that are in the middle. I consider them average.*
>
> *I'll watch to see if anybody in this group will dig*

deep and show me something that's worth me sticking my name on and recommending them to the team."

Wow. I had never thought of it quite that way, but Jeff had nailed it. You can be among the best of the best within your peer group, but if you're not excelling, overreaching, being better than, achieving more, being unique or taking the risk that no one else is willing to take, *you're still just average*. You won't make the cut.

YOU ARE NOT THAT SPECIAL

You might be thinking to yourself, "I'm not average. I earned a lot of money last year. I sit in the big corner office on the top floor. Do you know who I am?! I'm one of the elite. I'm special!"

First of all, congratulations. And, what Jim made perfectly clear is that there is average even among the elite. No matter what group, there is always a top, middle and bottom.

Every elite business professional, sales professional, entrepreneur or athlete I've worked with could name their area of average. He or she knew that within their respective peer group they had areas where they were in the top, middle or bottom. And they wanted to get to the top in every area of their professional and personal life.

Think of it this way. Let's say you are a human resources director or a department manager who is recruiting for the perfect candidate. Two hundred resumes are submitted. You sort through and pull out the top five candidates from the stack. Within those top five candidates, there is a top, middle and a bottom.

Let's do another example. Ask any teacher of a class of highly gifted students; he or she will tell you that there is still a top, middle and bottom within the gifted class. There is average among the gifted.

Consider whether you actually have made it to the top. You have zero competition. There is no one else better than you. There is still a top, middle and bottom within your personal performance. The real competition is you challenging you to perform at the next highest level.

How will you challenge yourself to be excellent? In what areas of your career, your performance and your personal life are you playing in the middle or in the bottom? You know you can do better. You know that there is more you are capable of achieving. Where can you challenge yourself to think, feel and behave at a higher level of excellence?

We all have areas of average. Areas where we can do better, be better, be more than we currently are at this moment. Observe yourself and find out where your areas exist.

JUST A NUMBER

When there is nothing to set individuals apart from their competition, nobody knows their name or gives a crap about them. They are not different. They are not better. They are not more efficient or effective. They are not innovative or creative. They are average.

If there are budget cuts in the company, they're out. In sports, if there is anyone who is even the slightest bit better than the person playing a position, that person is out and the next guy is in. It's business, baby!

Take an average entrepreneur as an example. If your

personality and performance blend in with all the other entrepreneurs who provide similar products or services, then you will only reach average success before you plateau.

You will constantly have to look over your shoulder to see who's creeping up or creeping in on your clients and your territory.

When a competing entrepreneur comes along and offers a new shiny object, clients will jump ship with little or no hesitation. One average entrepreneur is just as good as the next average entrepreneur.

It's simple: Average equals expendable. Average reduces people to being a number. As Donald Trump would say, "You're fired!" No reason required. It might be sad, but it's also true.

MAKING THE CUT

This is your first opportunity to break out of average. It is one of many opportunities to be bold, ballsy and completely honest with your Self.

Don't hold back. It takes courage to admit to areas and situations that have kept you stuck in average. It is also necessary for improvement, growth and moving into excellence.

Identify areas where you have been putting up with pain and denying yourself the opportunity to be excellent. Be specific. Remember, pain is a great motivator. Use it to your advantage.

1. In what areas are you currently accepting average? Where do you feel some pain? Where you are denying excellence?

   a. Career

   b. Home

   c. Relationships

   d. Finances

   e. Other

2. How can you challenge your Self in each of those areas?

   a. Career

   b. Home

c. Relationships

d. Finances

e. Other

3. What is the benefit you will experience when you challenge your Self and succeed in each of these areas?

a. Career

b. Home

c. Relationships

d. Finances

e. Other

CHAPTER TWO

No Excuse
for Average

If you quit ONCE it becomes a habit.
Never quit!!

— Michael Jordan

KEEP PUTTING IT UP

Michael Jordan never stopped shooting just because he missed shots. He knew that if you lose your touch, you don't give up or give in. You keep shooting until your touch comes back.

Michael's quote is very clear about the danger of quitting. Quitting once is not a big deal. But average people build addictive habits for quitting. They give in and give up too much, too often, and too fast. It's a harmful habit that must be broken.

GET OVER IT

Have you ever given up? Thrown in the towel? Waved that white flag and said, "enough"? We all have. We're human. It happens. Get over it. I really mean it: *Get Over It!*

Get over it FAST! There is a real danger in repeating the defeatist types of thoughts, behaviors and feelings that are associated with quitting.

NO ACCEPTABLE EXCUSE

There is no acceptable excuse for allowing self-defeating habits to take control of your career, life, health or relationships. There really isn't.

An addiction is simply a repeated pattern. It can be a pattern for success, happiness, health and even winning. It can be a pattern for failure, misery, blame and quitting. It's just a repeated pattern. Simple.

Addictive patterns are made up of how someone thinks, feels and behaves. If you think crappy thoughts, you will have emotions that support those crappy thoughts. Your crappy thoughts and emotions are followed by crappy behavior.

You can pretty much guess what crappy behaviors create. You got it. Crappy results. Let's not forget the consequences that go right along with results … they're crappy, too!

Then the cycle starts all over again. More crappy thoughts about the crappy results you just got! It's a downward spiral. At that point, you are pretty much screwed . . . unless, like Michael says, you never quit!

NEVER QUIT

You've got to keep shooting the ball so you don't lose your touch! That's what "never quit" means. Crap happens all the time. Every moment of every day, there are many opportunities to screw up, give in and give up. So what!

Persistence and commitment pay off. Get clear about what you want and go after it. Don't expect perfection. That's stupid, impractical and unreasonable. Simply stay focused on results and go after those results until you get them.

Great golfers know this. They play one shot at a time. If they have a poor shot, they recover quickly. Then they refocus their attention and find a way to make the next shot one of the best shots they have ever hit.

Here is another helpful hint to never giving up. A kid who falls down when learning to ride a bike is encouraged to get back up and go again. Kids need that extra encouragement. Adults seem to forget that part of the lesson. They can preach it, but have trouble following it in their own life.

Adults who learn how to encourage and praise themselves when they do well will greatly increase their chances of staying in the game and never quitting. They will be much more successful.

Don't create patterns of quitting right before you get what you really want. Not only will you get struck in average, you will be robbed of the thrill of conquering what you consider to be difficult or even seems impossible.

DON'T QUIT ON YOU

There are so many ways we can quit on ourselves. Little moments that can become bigger moments. We create patterns of thoughts, emotions and behaviors that become a habit of quitting. We begin to expect less of ourselves.

My junior year in high school, I read the *Cliff Notes* for *Moby Dick*. I really thought I had gotten away with something. I was quite proud of myself, until I received my grade. The 'C' on my book report let me know I had failed. My grade wasn't failing. I had failed at being the best that I could. I failed me.

I typically earned "A"s. This time, I had expected and accepted less of myself. Seems like a small thing, but the memory is still vivid. I felt embarrassed, sad, hurt and disappointed. I had let myself down.

Those small things can set patterns of quitting if they are not caught and changed. And they can crop up in later years in hurtful ways.

I quit on me when I stayed far too long in a relationship that was verbally and emotionally abusive. I thought I could fix "him." Then I finally figured out that "he" wasn't a science project for me to fix.

The freedom, power and courage I felt the day I kicked him out of my house and out of my life was incredible. It felt like I could breathe again.

I continue to keep my awareness up so I can quickly recognize when and where I might be cheating myself out of having more, being more, achieving more and getting more of what I want. It's important for all of us.

Where have you been cheating yourself? What have you accepted that is stealing your happiness? Draining your power?

Replacing old ways of thinking with bolder and more powerful thoughts leads to greater confidence and clarity. Old, sissy behaviors become ballsy behaviors. You are now focused on results.

It can be a bit scary at first, but diving into new circumstances and situations is exciting and rewarding.

CLIFF DIVING

Each and every time I faced the possibility of jumping into a new circumstance or situation, I would face old, familiar feelings. A new position, new job, new company or industry would set off a sweet mixture of fear, anxiety, worry and excitement. They consumed me.

Thoughts spun around in my head. Then the internal questions began: *"Do I? Don't I? What will happen if I do?"*

Here we go again. The great debate. *"If I don't do it, how can I face myself? I won't be able to look myself in the mirror tomorrow if I turn this down. Crap, just do it! I can't NOT do it. That would be worse."*

Holy man, I knew what was about to happen next: *"Damn it, here I go again. I Got This!"*

I would be off on a new adventure. You would think I was about to dive off an actual cliff. It felt like it. It felt like I was putting my life in real danger.

When you are on the cliff of making a decision—a big career or life-changing decision—it can be scary. The debates and doubts can take over and cause you to recoil back into average.

Don't quit. The more often you push yourself to jump into opportunities, the more quickly you build trust. You will trust the exhilaration you are feeling. It will propel you into greater and greater success. The evidence will prove you right.

True competitors love this feeling. When others are scared, they are excited. They know that others are about to fall back in their dust. Get lost in the crowd. Competitors know they are about to win. They enjoy knowing they have a competitive edge.

Top competitors learn to remain courageous when frightened. They become even more focused under extreme pressure.

They know that quitting will create a repeated pattern of quitting. And that winning will create a repeated pattern of winning. They choose to win!

QUITTING IS NOT AN OPTION

Opportunities are waiting for you. Dig deep. Be raw and be real. Identify where and when any addictive thoughts and behaviors show up.

Then—and this is critical—identify what action you will take to replace those behaviors with bolder and ballsier thoughts and behaviors.

Don't judge. Act like a detective and just note the facts.

1. List any situations or circumstances when you quit, gave in or gave up.

2. What would you have done differently, knowing what you know now?

3. Looking at your answer to question #2, what would you have to be thinking to support your new actions?

4. If you knew you could trust yourself to win in these circumstances or situations, how would you feel?

CHAPTER THREE

No Sissies Allowed

I'm a dude playing a dude
disguised as another dude.
— Robert Downey Jr., as Kirk Lazarus
in the movie *Tropic Thunder*

STOP LOOKING AT ME

I love the movie *Tropic Thunder*. When I heard the above line by Kirk Lazarus, I thought it was the perfect way to describe how average people live their lives. That one simple sentence says so much.

Average people don't want to be seen, heard or exposed for their weaknesses. They hide out. A disguise is the perfect cover-up.

I'm curious whether you have ever met someone like this. They seem to have a different personality for every occasion: one for business, one for home, one for vacations and another for when they are out with friends. Whew, that's exhausting. Sound like anyone you know?

I get it. We all have the urge to fit in, be liked and feel comfortable. It seems only natural. It's also average behavior.

If ho-humming it through life and staying average is the goal, then disguises totally work. In fact, it's a perfect plan for mediocrity.

Are you going to play up to your strengths
or down to other people's weaknesses?
– Deborah Dubree

I WAS A SISSY

I have behaved like a sissy. I freely admit it. I was hiding out when I was a receptionist. I bought into society's opinion that my capabilities were weak and therefore I must be weak too. Plus, I had decided that my personal value was tied to the size of my paycheck.

Who was I, anyway? I was just a young girl from a little town outside of Chicago. When it came time to fill out a job application, under the question about my level of education, the only thing I could write was "high school diploma." Not much to work with there. I bought into the disguise of "I am not enough."

To give you an example of how naïve I was, on the job application for receptionist, there was a space to fill in the hourly rate that I was hoping to be paid. I had no idea what to write.

Before starting to look for a job, I had calculated exactly what I needed to meet the additional expenses of childcare, extra car, gas and miscellaneous expenses.

Then, I took the total of those expenses and came up with an hourly rate. That way, I knew what I had to earn just to break even.

That carefully calculated amount was what I listed on the application. I didn't want to risk not getting the job, so I decided not to ask for any more money than what was necessary to cover my bills.

When I was offered the position, I still remember the manager who hired me saying, "We only have one problem." My heart sank. He continued, "We can't pay you what you're asking for on the application"—big pause—"because it's less than the legal minimum wage."

For real! Are you kidding me! I was so embarrassed. Honestly, I didn't even know there was such a thing as a legal minimum wage.

Looking back on my career, it's funny that someone who couldn't figure out her own pay rate would eventually become a construction accountant, accounting manager, chief financial officer and even an entrepreneur who would troubleshoot the financial status of at-risk companies. Clearly, I was hiding out behind a mask.

For the next six months, I kept my mouth shut and my head down and just did my damn job. Then I got bored. The responsibilities of receptionist weren't enough for me. I didn't feel challenged. It wasn't exciting or rewarding.

When the position of construction accountant opened up right in front of me, I really wanted it. It would give me the opportunity to be more and have more. The additional money would come in really handy. The chance to achieve more both excited and scared me.

Now keep in mind, I knew nothing about accounting. I had absolutely no construction experience. I was not remotely qualified to apply for, and much less fill, this new position, and I knew it. Those were the facts. It was painful to have the opportunity so close and know it wasn't possible.

For two weeks, I felt stuck between what I wanted and what I thought I was capable of having. The deadline for turning in résumés was fast approaching. I was in pure agony. Every day and every night, I suffered with the thoughts of what the new position meant to me. What it could do for my family and me.

Then there was the mail. Every single day, I dreaded opening the mail. There were always several highly qualified résumés for the new position. I hated it. I wanted to throw them in the trash, but I didn't.

As applicants started coming in for interviews, I had to smile nicely, greet them and act like I was glad they were there. I wasn't! It pissed me off.

I knew the obvious decision was to just be grateful for what I had, settle in and do my job. And there were lots of outside opinions to remind me that I was average.

Caring friends said I should forget about the position. They said things like, "Why would you want to put yourself through that? You know it's going to hurt like hell when they turn you down. Just forget it."

I agreed. I mean, who in their right mind would knowingly set themselves up to be disappointed, hurt and even embarrassed? I wouldn't. Or would I?

THE WALL

This is the exact point where average people get stuck. It can feel like there is a wall that keeps them from getting what they really want. A big, thick, broad and tall wall of fear, frustration, overwhelm, worry, disappointment and even anger.

Telling yourself you can get over, under, around or through the emotional wall doesn't work. There is an incessant internal dialogue of *"I can"* and *"I will."* These are immediately followed by, *"No you can't"* and *"You're crazy to even try."*

Average people back down, shut down and take the sissy way out when this happens. Their emotions keep them limited and settling for less. They think that hiding out is easier. It's not!

Hiding out is a slow, painful and agonizing existence. Action makes the difference. Action changes everything!

JUMP . . . FEET-FIRST

I hit my own emotional wall and stayed there for nearly two weeks. With only two days left before the deadline, I turned in my poor excuse for a résumé. I tucked it in the middle of the other résumés that had arrived in the mail that day.

Sheepishly walking over to the construction manager's office, I laid the stack of résumés on his desk. I was so scared.

When it came time for my interview, I didn't know what to say. The construction manager was the same man I had spoken to and joked with every day during my six months as receptionist. But this was different.

I had watched how he worked. He ran a tight ship. He was a good leader. And he was fair. He also had a "no bullshit" attitude when it came to work. I liked and respected him.

At one point during the interview, he asked me point-blank, "Would you have any problem performing the responsibilities listed on this job description?"

The freakin' job description was three pages long! My eyes blurred when I turned the pages and pretended to read it. I saw words like debit, credit, work-in-progress. I had no idea what they meant. At that moment, I made a decision. It was time to tell a lie!

I took a breath, squared myself up in the chair, looked him directly in the eyes and firmly stated, "Absolutely not!"

The minute the words came out of my mouth, I almost gasped at my boldness. *"Holy crap, what have I just done?"* I held my breath and waited. He thanked me, and that was that.

I wanted to run but held myself together long enough to shake his hand and return to my desk. I had made it through the interview. For now, that was all I could do.

That night I told my husband, "When I looked at that job description, I didn't even know what some of those words meant, much less how to do them. But they said they would train the person they hire." This was my feeble attempt to make myself feel better. To let myself know that all would be okay.

I had made one ballsy move. All I could do now was wait. My fate was in the hands of someone else. This was and still is a feeling I hate.

BET ON YOU

When I was offered the position, I couldn't believe it. That bold decision to turn in my crappy little unqualified résumé changed the trajectory of my entire personal and professional life. I had reset the baseline of who I was and who I would become. I had taken a huge risk. The payoff was far greater than I could have imagined at the time.

The entire experience taught me Ten Guidelines I still live by today:

1. People bet on YOU first, your knowledge second.
2. Speak with authority and people listen.
3. Others won't believe in you until you believe in yourself.
4. Don't ever take yourself out of the game. Jump in. Force others to pull you out.
5. Push the limits of your capabilities and then figure out a way to make good on your promises.
6. Being afraid is human. Taking courageous action is a decision.
7. Stop listening to others' opinions. You know what is best for you.
8. Smart people ask questions. Stupid people think they know it all.
9. Limit your agony by making quick decisions.
10. Guts and grit rule!

My decisions continue to push my buttons and push my limits. I like taking on a challenge and conquering it. It is exciting, rewarding and fulfilling.

Taking risks and jumping in feet-first, along with being bold and taking ballsy actions, became part of my business strategy and plan for success. I refused to be a sissy. I learned to bet on me!

When you make a bold, ballsy decision,
you'd better back it up with the right action!
– Deborah Dubree

After working through the time of my two-week notice for the receptionist position, I moved over to the construction division of the company. It was now time to fulfill my promise that I could perform the new responsibilities.

My fear quickly changed. I was afraid of making a fool of myself. I was terrified of not being able to do the job. My fear intensified. What if I screwed things up and got fired? I'd be out of a job altogether. *Oh, crap!* What had I done?

I struggled to learn the construction terms, putting in the long hours and keeping up with the fast pace.

But each morning, I would get up and go after it again. My early-morning daily ritual became a way to pump up the volume on my courage.

While standing in front of the bathroom mirror, I would apply my makeup. My warrior paint. With every stroke of color, I felt stronger, had more courage and knew that I could go out and conquer another battle.

Firmly planting my bare feet shoulder-width apart on the cold bathroom floor, I would tell myself that no one would push me over or push me around.

During my daily commute to work, I endured bitter and heated arguments. This was a bit unsettling for the other drivers on the road, since I was the only one in my car.

The good news was I always won the debate. And I made sure that by the time I pulled into the parking lot, the bold, ballsy me was fully in charge.

During the following eighteen-month period, I earned three raises. Setting the bar high and reaching it felt really good. I wanted to and needed to do it again. I vowed never to play average again.

Being average and acting like a sissy sucks. That's a problem. Getting stuck in average is a much bigger problem. Sometimes the only way to get unstuck is to take a deep breath and jump . . . feet-first . . . into action! The results can be life-changing.

SAD, AVERAGE, FATAL

It's sad, it's average and it's fatal to keep doing what you've always done. There is zero satisfaction, excitement, challenge or glory in it. There are no stories to share with friends and family. No stories to include in books.

When others ask, "What have you been up to lately?" The sad, average and fatal answer is, "Oh, not much!"

At that point, just throw in the towel. You're barely breathing. There's only a slight hint of a pulse. You're about to flat-line.

Action Trumps Fear
– Deborah Dubree

Action will start the competitive juices flowing and get the heart pumping. Action trumps fear. Action opens up the opportunity for courage, faith and trust to take over. Action will help you push the limits of limited thinking and prod you into pushing your capabilities to the next level.

Make a decision and take the first step into action. Once you make that first step, then the second and third steps will each become easier. The first step is always the most difficult one.

Push yourself. Don't let other people ruin your fun, your progress or your career. This is your life, not theirs.

When I made the decision to go on a great white shark dive, friends told me I was crazy. They reminded me of the movie *Jaws* and even felt compelled to hum the catchy theme music from the movie for my listening pleasure. I was not amused!

One of my friends finally asked me why I would jump into a cage, in freezing water, with fourteen-foot sharks swimming under me, at me and around me. My answer was simple, "Because I've never done it before!"

Too often, people would rather lower the floor than raise the bar of possibilities and opportunities. There is zero growth potential in stagnation. Excellence is at the top. It does not exist at the bottom or even in the mediocre, middle level.

Do something that you have never ever done before. Push the limits in your personal and your business lives. When you go beyond reasonable and possible in one area, the other area receives the full advantage also.

My shark dive was for personal fun and to push my personal boundaries. It also provided me even greater courage to push the boundaries in my professional life.

You are one person. The experiences you have, the knowledge that you gain and the growth you realize in one area of your life cannot be separated from the other areas of your life.

Oh, by the way . . . You don't have to like what you experience when you push the limits. You don't even have to be good at it. When you are attempting something for the first time, why would you expect to be good? It's something that is new and different. Cut yourself some slack.

If you try something new and don't like it, don't do it again. Pretty simple. Still look at what you learned from the experience. Just don't do it again.

If you discover that you really like doing it, then you can practice and perfect your skills.

Remember this. Once you get really good at something, it's time to raise the bar. Push your limits again and again. Reset your baseline one more time. Excellence is a pursuit. Don't ever stop pursuing it.

My personal mantra became, "If I can do THAT, what else can I do?" Each time my baseline of experience, knowledge, talent, skill, courage and confidence grew, I knew I had the ability to go out and achieve more, do more and be more. It was time to reach for even greater heights.

Each time you push your limits and accomplish something you have not accomplished in the past, it's important to set a new baseline. Recognize that you are not the same person you were before you conquered this goal. You know more than you did before. You have accomplished more, learned new skills and exemplified greater courage.

Don't stop. Going with the excitement is being on the edge of growth. You are standing on the edge of another level of excellence. Master where you are, and then jump again.

Always be sure to give yourself some props! Celebrate what you have just accomplished. Remember where you were and how far you have come. You have earned the right to be successful. You deserve the success.

Now, go do something else that scares the crap out of you!

TIME TO JUMP!

Jumping into action does not mean you have to run out and book a great white shark dive. That's the kind of stuff I do. I'm not you and you're not me.

Jumping into action means you look at your current circumstances, situations, relationships, personality traits and any other area that could use some upgrades.

Then ask yourself some questions. Remember, this is not about judging, lamenting or criticizing. Those are useless habits that waste a lot of time and energy.

Go grab a piece of paper and something to write with. As you ask each question, write down everything that comes into your mind. The more you write, the better! Superficial bullshit answers can be sorted out later. For now, just write.

Making bold decisions and taking ballsy action starts by identifying where average currently exists. Get raw and get real. Your money, career, legacy, life, respect, recognition and what you want most in life are hanging in the balance. That's all!

Begin with these two questions:

1. Where does average exists in your career and in your life?

2. In what areas will you push your limits and take action?

Examples:

- Maybe you've been floating by at work and it's time to really show up and go for that position that has always seemed just out of your reach.

- Maybe there is a relationship that needs to be improved or removed.

- Will you set a sales quota that feels beyond your current capabilities?

- You could pick a place or situation where you will speak in front of a group, knowing that it scares the crap out of you.

- Will you tell loved ones why they matter to you, when opening up is something that has made you uncomfortable in the past?

- Set up a schedule to have more meaningful conversations with your kids. And do it more often.

- Clean up areas of your life that you have been ignoring and hoping would simply go away.

Use these next two questions to go deeper and examine any disguises you have been wearing. Look over the answers you have already identified from doing the previous exercise and ask yourself:

1. In what areas are you hiding out?

2. Where have you been playing it safe?

It's time to take action

Look over your list of answers and ask the following questions to set up a successful and doable action plan.

1. Where will you jump into action feet-first? Pick just one.

2. What specific steps <u>will</u> you take right now? (Note: I didn't say what action *might* you take.)

   - List your action steps below in the appropriate category.

   - Pick one or two steps per week and jump into action. You will be glad that you did.

     1. Work:

     2. Home:

     3. Relationships:

     4. Finances:

     5. Other:

BEWARE: Average people will find ways to fool themselves into thinking that they are taking meaningful action when they are not. Just because you are in motion does not mean you are taking action that will move you out of average and into excellence. Think of it this way.

You can jump up and down ...
action with zero benefit.

You can jump off ...
a form of giving up or giving in. No benefit.

You can jump back ...
Stop it. Really, stop it.

You can jump feet- first ...
This is challenging, scary as hell and
extremely rewarding!

It's All Action.
The difference is in the direction you move.

YOU choose!!

CHAPTER FOUR

Stop Pissy Sissy Behaviors

BOTTOM LINE

So here we go. I'm taking all of your excuses away. Breaking out of average starts with becoming aware of average behaviors.

Below is a list of 10 Pissy Sissy Behaviors that I have identified from observing what gets in the way of excellence. I'm sure you can come up with other behaviors to add to the list. I encourage you to go for it. The more that are identified, the better.

Answer the questions with each behavior. Then, take action to stop your own PISSY SISSY BEHAVIORS! The danger if you don't is that you keep hanging onto average and hanging out in average.

The opportunity to make a new choice happens moment to moment. Choices are everywhere. And every choice you make has its own set of behaviors that will lead to results. Those results lead to consequences.

Make the wrong choice and you have to endure the crappy results and consequences. Make the right choice and you have the enjoyment of celebrating the results and the consequences. The bad and good news about all that . . . the choice is always up to you!

10 PISSY SISSY BEHAVIORS

1. **Tell Me A Story:** Always having a ready-made excuse or story about why you can't do what you know you could or should do. Stories and excuses roll off your tongue with ease because you have had way too much practice.

   I was about to make the client calls, but got really busy with this other project. I'll call them tomorrow, okay?

   Mommy, I'll pick up my toys next time, I promise. I'm too tired to do it now.

   – Have you ever made up an excuse or story to get out of doing something you didn't want to do or felt uncomfortable doing?

   – What's your plan for changing this type of behavior in the future?

2. **Give 'Em The Finger:** You blame and complain about people, circumstance and situations. It's easier than admitting you could or should be acting differently. Taking personal responsibility to change your own circumstances it out of the question. And, you complain that someone else (anybody but you!) should do something. Pointing fingers at everyone else has become an annoying habit.

   I know I was going to have it to you today, but Darren didn't give me the report in time for me to get my analysis done. It's his fault I didn't get it done. You understand, right?

   I know it's wrong, but that's what Brenda told me to do.

- When is the last time you blamed others instead of taking personal responsibility? What was the result?

- What is your plan for changing this type of behavior in the future?

3. **Good As It Gets:** *"Hey, I'm successful. I'm comfortable. What more do you want?"* These types have reached a comfortable level of success and then level off. This is the ho-humming, status quo and flat-lined performer.

This is a really sneaky one, since they might still be working long hours and showing up at meetings. If they play sports, they are still performing like they have in the past. But they are not doing more. Not pushing the boundaries. Not excelling into new levels of excellence.

I made my sales quota for the past six months; what more do you want? It's more than anybody else is doing!

- Where are you playing it safe? Settling for status quo?

- What's your plan for changing this type of behavior in the future?

4. **You Owe Me:** The holier-than-thou, egotistical, the-world-owes-me "entitlement" sobs of "You Owe Me." They think that just because they have reached a certain level of success (or their mammas or daddies have), they're special. They are wrong. They are sissies. And they are stupid. So there!

As I checked into the resort, I overheard her in the distance. Jewelry dripping from her neck, ears and hands, she shrieked commands at the bellman. "Stop banging my luggage around. Do you have any idea how much that costs? You better not park my car where it will get scratched." And on and on.

- Has this ever been you? Have you ever acted "holier than thou?" Ever put someone in his or her place verbally or with your stare or glance? Be honest.

- What's your plan for changing this type of behavior in the future?

5. **That's Settled:** Settling for average jobs, average positions, average pay and average results. Conforming to the rules, don't rock the boat, and never rattle the cage. They become a good little doobie.

I know I would be better than X (fill in the name) at that position, but I'm not qualified. I don't think I could do it.

I'm just going to keep my head down, do my job and hope that nobody bothers me. I'm doing okay.

- Have you settled into your current company or position? Are you really comfortable, yet not completely satisfied? Would you like to shake things up?

- What's your plan for changing this type of behavior in the future?

6. **Idly By:** Refusing to speak up when they disagree with policies or people. They shut up and shut down. Disagreeing is uncomfortable. Others determine their fate, while they sit idly by.

Have you ever been to a restaurant and received a crappy meal? Maybe the steak was not cooked like you requested. Or you ordered a side salad and they brought you fries instead.

- Did you complain? Send it back? Make them correct the problem?

  Or did you take what they gave you and felt horrible the entire meal. You complained to your family or friends that the service was bad, but did nothing to actually correct the issue?

- How does this type behavior affect other areas of you professional and personal life?

- What's your plan for changing this type of behavior in the future?

7. **Cover Up:** Procrastinate, hesitate, deliberate and hibernate when faced with a challenge. It's much more comfortable to pull the covers up over their heads when they feel overwhelmed, confused and frustrated.

   I felt hurt when X (fill in the name of a family member, friend, co-worker, mentor) said that to me. But I don't want to say anything. I'll be alright.

   Getting up and speaking would really raise my credibility, but it scares the crap out of me. Someday I'll get up the nerve to do it.

   - When is the last time you hid out? Didn't want to be seen or heard?

   - Where were you? What were you thinking? What were you worried about or thought would happen if you stood up or stood out?

    – What's your plan for changing this type of behavior in the future?

8. **I Don't Know:** When asked for an opinion, they respond with "I don't know." Or they give a response that is so vague, it's meaningless. Taking a stand for what they believe in doesn't happen. Even giving an unsolicited opinion is out of the question.

   Getting people to speak their minds and give honest opinions was one of the most difficult obstacles I faced in business. Everyone is afraid of offending someone. They would rather sit quietly than speak their minds.

    – What about you? Can you remember a time in your professional or in your personal life when you stayed quiet when you really wanted to speak up?

    – What was your biggest fear or reason for hesitation?

    – What's your plan for changing this type of behavior in the future?

9. **Buying In:** They buy-in to their current situation, education, circumstances and mindset . . . believing that they're stuck, limited and out of options.

   A very bright staff accountant became frustrated with being in her position. She shared with me that she wanted to become a project coordinator.

   When I asked Donna what she was doing to make that happen, she said, "I don't have the knowledge to ever fill that position. No one would take me serious."

   With encouragement, she spoke with the general field

foreman. Once he heard about Donna's desire, he put a plan in place to teach her what she needed to know. She was surprised, thrilled and jumped at the opportunity. Donna became one of the best project coordinators we ever had.

- Have you ever given up on yourself? Accepted limitations as a definition of what you were capable of being or achieving?

- What's your plan for changing this type of behavior in the future?

10. **Whatever:** They do what anybody else in their position would do. No more. They have been lulled into a mediocre state of "whatever."' How sad and disappointing for them!

Have you ever "called it in"? Did as little as possible? Pretended to do more that you were actually doing?

We all have at some point. Just before vacation. When you have given two weeks' notice. Or when you become bored or frustrated with things.

What about your personal life. Have you ever slacked off in your relationships with family and friends? Have you ever kind-of listened to your children when they really needed your full attention?

- When have you "called it in" and not given your best?

- How has that behavior affected other areas of your life?

- What's your plan for changing this type of behavior in the future?

CHAPTER FIVE

Stand Up
or Shut Up

Knowing the cost of staying stuck in average is important. But knowledge alone is just good table-talk. You can impress your friends with the new knowledge, but your life doesn't change a damn bit.

My hope is that something you have read so far may feel like it hit way too close to home. You might feel a bit scared, excited or even concerned. You might even feel a bit ticked off.

Good for you. What you are feeling signifies progress. The mixture of feelings means you are about to break into a new level of excellence, but only if you take action.

There is an excitement in the air. You're at a point of decision. What's it going to be?

STAND UP or SHUT UP

It's time to stand up and jump . . . feet-first . . . into breaking the addiction to average and move into excellence. Or shut up and go back to average. Your choice.

When the decision is to stand up, take control and get more of what you want, you create a greater competitive edge. You will execute with confidence, courage and consistency.

The payoff is huge!

BREAK THE ADDICTION

I began this section stating that average is an addiction. That accepting average is accepting failure.

Have you completed the exercises in this section? If not, why not? I really mean it. Knowing why you didn't do the exercises is a very important question for you to explore and answer.

In completing the exercises, here is an overview of what you have discovered.

1. Quitting is not an option. You identified where you have quit in the past. And what bold decisions and ballsy actions you will take now.

2. Pain is a motivator. You listed where you have been putting up with pain and denying yourself opportunities. And what you can do to challenge yourself. Also, the benefits of challenging yourself.

3. Time to jump. You wrote down where average currently exists in your performance, your career and your life … along with an action plan to make a change.

4. To take away any excuses, you finally named any Sissy Pissy Behaviors and began to challenge and change those behaviors.

LET'S DO THIS!

The 3 "R"s to Break an Addiction
Recognize – Replace - Remember

Step One: Recognize

You have already completed this step. You have recognized and admitted that there is an addiction to average in one or more areas of your performance, career or life. Choose one area that is a priority. Focus on it first before moving on to the others.

Step Two: Replace

Remember the formula we discussed in the beginning?

Average thoughts equals average behaviors.

Average behaviors lead to average results.

Average results are followed by average consequences.

To break an addictive behavior requires that these three areas be replaced. Thoughts, behaviors and the accompanying emotions are a package deal. Attempting to change one, without the others, will lead to short-term results. Then, you're right back to average.

Ask and answer the following questions: What is the behavior you want to replace? What is the new, desirable replacement behavior? Be specific.

What do you need to be thinking to achieve the new behavior? What emotions will best support the new thinking and the new behavior?

Write down your answers to all the questions. Be exact. Then take the necessary actions to make the change.

Step Three: Remember

- Remember the pain you experienced from the old behaviors, old thoughts and old emotions. Pain is a motivator.

- Remember to watch carefully for any average thoughts, emotions and behaviors that attempt to creep back in and keep you in average. Catch them quickly.

Then begin the cycle again. Go right back to Recognize, Replace and Remember. This is your new cycle for success in breaking the addiction to average and moving into excellence.

Bonus R: Repeat – Repeat – Repeat

New successful behaviors, thoughts and emotions must be repeated and repeated and repeated. Always remain focused on the desired results.

Keep in mind that it takes a lot to get back on track if old behaviors, thoughts and emotions are allowed to squirm their way back into your daily habits. You will slip back to being average.

An alcoholic doesn't pick up a drink, have a sip and state, "It was just a little sip. No big deal. I'm fine." If you are a lover of chocolate, ice cream or breads (oh wait that's me) you know how difficult it is to just have a little bit.

Addictive average thoughts, emotions and behaviors are the same. Have a few of them and you'll be having more and more.

Sustaining excellence and achieving greater success requires commitment and consistency. Plan for events, situations, people, places and times that could trip you up and take you out. Practice how you will behave, feel and think the next time. Repeat the new thoughts, emotions and behaviors until they become your new habit.

NO LONGER NUMB
AND DUMB

Don't do what everybody else is doing.
Do what works!

– Deborah Dubree

Smart people who become addicted to average go numb and dumb. They give up on their ambition, drive, guts, determination, commitment and everything else necessary to get ahead.

When they give up on their hopes and dreams of achieving excellence, they feel self-disappointment and disgust. They have to numb out to survive.

They also dumb themselves down in an attempt to fit in. They act dumb, do dumb things and say dumb stuff. They try to fit in and blend in when they could and should be standing out.

It doesn't work. It is not satisfying. It's just sad.

This section covers how to stop doing what others do and start doing what actually works.

Numb and dumb is not a plan for success.
— **Deborah Dubree**

CHAPTER SIX

Goals
Don't Matter

Everyone is supposed to have goals, right? Clear, obtainable, big, over-arching, audacious goals. Without goals, people are doomed to failure. Scary things will happen. You're destined to be out on the street, pushing a shopping cart and looking for a warm place to sleep. Boxes start to look like home.

Experts state that to be successful, it's important to start with a goal. Well, all the experts except me. Some goals just don't matter.

IF YOU'RE AVERAGE, YOUR GOALS DON'T MATTER

Those who are average can set all the goals they want, but their goals don't matter. They are not going to be achieved anyway. Average people take average actions. Average actions bring average results. With average results, your goals disappear, along with hopes and dreams. Back to being average. It's a shame and it's a waste.

I know, I know. People try to accomplish goals. They really do. They want to make a change. They want to get better and achieve more. Too much wanting and not enough achieving!

We see it all the time. After a few days or weeks or months, they go right back to their old ways. Nothing has changed.

Well, almost nothing. When their goals crash and burn, so does their opinion of themselves.

A common theme occurs every New Year's Eve. Goals are set to lose weight, quit smoking, eat healthier, exercise more, find the perfect new job, stay more connected with friends and family. The list goes on and on.

When those goals go unmet, people feel worse off than they did before they set the goals. They feel upset, frustrated and more disappointed than ever. They feel like losers.

They begin to wonder what else they're going to fail at. They stay stuck and they stay average. Then, the pattern repeats itself.

WHO GIVES A CRAP

Another problem is setting goals that don't matter and acting as if someone should care. The *"who really gives a crap"* type of goals.

When Rita, a sales professional, excitedly told me that she had set a sales goal to close $3.5 million in contracts during the next quarter, I was impressed for a moment.

Then I asked Rita what her sales had been over the previous two quarters. I quickly became unimpressed. The $3.5 million was an average quarterly closing rate for her, based on the previous six months of actual sales closed.

Rita had called her sales quota a goal. It really wasn't. It was simply a regurgitation of what she was already doing.

For many, the $3.5 million would have been a huge goal. But Rita was fooling herself by thinking it was a goal. It was not bigger, better or more fulfilling than what she had repeatedly accomplished.

Setting and accomplishing an attainable average goal is simply doing what you have always done. Writing it down doesn't make it a goal. What you really have is a task.

You have a realistic daily task that is great for a "to do" list. Set the task, complete it and mark it off the list. *Good job!*

Stay awake and aware. If a goal is too easy, it might feel good for a moment. *"Woo hoo, look what I did!"* Then reality creeps back in. You realize what you really accomplished was a task.

The "who really gives a crap" goals are a great way to dodge the big challenges, dreams and aspirations. It's a way to dodge what really matters. It's a way to numb out and dumb down.

Goals are meant to stretch, push and motivate people past their current capabilities and achievements. They prod you to act with greater and greater courage. Goals don't lower the floor; they raise the bar.

GOALS ARE SIMPLE

Too much focus has been put on goal setting. Even high-achieving, competitive business professional and athletes are way too focused on goals. Goals are simple. Here's a highly simplified sample of goals I hear when I initially ask my clients what they want to achieve:

- Football players: Play better, harder and more consistently
- Golfers: Lower my score
- Entrepreneurs: Make more money
- Sales experts: Close more sales
- Business professionals: Outsmart my competition

Really pay attention. It's important to understand the nuances of what I'm about to lay out in this next part.

What most experts suggest, right after someone has set his or her goal, is an action plan. Experts may switch up the wording or the order of these steps, but the steps are pretty much the same. The conversation goes something like this:

1. By what date do you want to achieve this goal? *Good*

2. What are the steps you need to take for you to reach your goal? *Nice*

3. What is the most important step to take first? *Excellent*

4. Let's put this on the calendar, timeline or map it out, so you can see what you have to do each month, week or day, to ensure you can accomplish your goal. *Perfect*

5. To ensure you achieve your goals, you and I will speak each week. I'll hold you accountable!!

There you have it. That should do it, right? There is a goal, actionable and attainable steps, a timeline and accountability. You're all set.

You're going to be a rock star! Make six figures! Win all your games!! Lower your golf score by five strokes! Right? Wrong, wrong, wrong!

A FIVE-YEAR-OLD CAN DO IT

The steps for setting goals and action plans are not rocket science. You could Google the steps, then find a friend to support you and to hold you accountable. Pretty easy stuff.

A five-year-old can even set goals and create an action plan.

Just ask them these questions, "What do you want?" Answer, *"I want to go play!"* "When do you want to go play?" *"NOW!"* "What do you have to do first before you can go play?" *"Eat my supper."*

There you go. Goal is set (go play). The plan is in place (eat supper). Timeline (now). It's all easy and attainable or so it seems!

All that is missing is the execution. The action. The "getting it done" part. Just one spoonful after the last spoonful until the plate is empty. Seems simple enough, right?

This is the exact point where all the whining, crying and backlash start. And that's just from the parents. Execution is crucial. Execution is where goals and plans fall apart.

> *Without execution, goals, plans, hopes and dreams become an exercise in frustration and disappointment.*
>
> **– Deborah Dubree**

Here's the deal—set goals. I do. My clients do. Goals and plans are important. Just don't complicate the process. The gold is in the execution. That is where the effort and focus should be placed.

ROCK YOUR WORLD

What is it that you want? Really want. What is the one thing, above all else, that would rock your world to the core if you earned it, owned it, could be it or could do it? Really get clear on this before you move into Chapter Seven on execution.

You can start small and move up. I started out my career that way and it all worked out fine. Or you can have one big, lifelong goal.

Some of my clients have had one long-term dream their entire life. A dream of playing in the NFL, being a pro golfer, becoming a lawyer or a high-paid executive. That's okay, too. If you have one big dream you want to fulfill, go for it. Take action.

Hopes, dreams and goals are different for everyone. The great part is, you get to choose.

No matter what your goal is, you must push your boundaries, your limits. It's time to get uncomfortable and know that you'll be okay.

Is there a performance record you want to shatter? Do you want to sell more? Have greater revenues. Higher profit margins. More return on your time or money investment. Attract more clients. Be less angry and more at ease. More assertive and less laid back.

How can you be the absolute best at what you do? Lower your score. Raise your score. Maybe you want to start something or stop something. Lose something or gain something. Lose anger and gain respect. Start smiling and stop yelling. Start speaking on a stage and stop procrastinating about it.

Choose something and see it through.

DON'T LET LUGGAGE GET IN YOUR WAY

I knew what I wanted. A trip to Africa had been on my "list of experiences" for a bunch of years. Not just a visit to the various countries of Africa. I wanted to fully experience the culture, the people, the animals and the land.

After selling my construction company, I knew it was time. My love for animals and adventure came together in one amazing and unforgettable trip.

What I am about to share with you is what happened on the final night after two weeks out in the bush. As you read this story, notice the lessons at every juncture. Where do you see yourself in the mix? What are the choices you would have made? What would have been your reaction or response. Be honest with yourself.

Our guide had gathered our group of seventeen together to give us final instructions for the morning departure. There was a lot of juggling of schedules to ensure we were all going to make our morning connections.

Once we were all clear and confident about the morning details, our guide offered us one final opportunity to drive out to the Maasai Mara region within the Serengeti Ecosystem of Africa.

We were tired. In the last thirteen days, we had traveled from Nairobi to Tanzania, visiting the Ngorongoro Crater, then over to Serengeti National Park in Tanzania and crossing over to the Kenya side of the Serengeti. And now we were in the Maasai Mara region.

Each morning we would wake up early. Grab our bug spray, hats and cameras before heading out on safari. Our goal was to catch sight of the wildlife that was still out from the night before. We had to catch them grazing and hunting before they began to hide from the intense heat of the day.

Late morning, it was back to camp and back to our tents. We would hide from the afternoon sun, too.

We ventured out of our tents in the late afternoon. Climbing into our open-air four-wheel-drive vehicles, we headed out on safari again. Bouncing across the hard ground, we hunted for any sign of life.

There were times we would sit for hours in one spot, with eyes peeled in every direction. Hoping to get a glimpse of life. Then someone would point and yell, "There, over there!" Off we would go, bumping and bouncing to get close enough for a glimpse and a picture of a lion, elephant, giraffe, hippo, leopard or rhino.

But on this last night, most of the group wanted to pack, chill out and prepared for the long flights home. Some, like myself, would be headed out to visit other areas of Africa.

Three in the group said yes to heading out on safari again. I said, "Hell, yes!" I mean really. We were only allowed thirty pounds of luggage for the entire two-week trip. That included all cameras, essentials and clothes. How long could it take to pack? Roll it up, stick it in the duffle bag and you're done!

I wanted to scream, "You're in the freakin' Serengeti, people! Just how often do you plan on having a trip of a lifetime?"

But isn't that what some people do? They stop short. Right before they get what they want, reach their goal or have an experience of a lifetime, they throw in the towel. They pack clothes instead having an adventure. They sit around and tell stories instead of being *in* the story.

The four of us climbed into the vehicle and headed out with our guide. Three men and me. Typical. We were laughing, making fun of each other and sharing some of our best photos from the days before.

For about thirty minutes, we drove around watching for signs of life. We saw various small animals, including an owl sitting all by itself in a dry, grassy patch in the middle of nowhere. Life was good.

Then our driver suddenly slammed on the brakes. "Do you see her? Look there. She has a baby with her, too!" Oh my gosh! It was a mamma black rhino and her baby.

This sighting was rare. There are only about 3,610 black rhinos left in the entire world. There were seventy-thousand in the late 1960s, before all of the killings.

We drove very slowly and quietly over to mamma and baby. They meandered along, stopping to eat from time to time, barely looking up. We all sat stunned.

This was an incredible sight. Snapping our pictures and whispering our excitement, we each knew at some deep level that this was a moment. A beautiful and rare moment in time. We all took a collective breath and took it all in.

When you say "yes" to possibilities before knowing how they will turn out, there can be rare, once-in-a-lifetime opportunities waiting for you to savor. But you have to learn to say "yes."

We stayed as long as we could, knowing we needed to beat the darkness back to camp. By now, we had driven WAY off the beaten path.

Our driver noticed clouds moving quickly in our direction. He began racing back toward the makeshift road. He knew that the road would help protect the vehicle from getting buried in the mud. But we didn't make it.

A fast-moving rain cloud engulfed us within minutes. Fast and hard, the rain pelted the canvas top and sides of our vehicle. The driver's view was completely blinded. We were stuck. Stuck in the mud.

Not one of us could get out of the vehicle to help push or dig away the mud to free the tires. Our guide warned us about the chance of wildlife that could leap out of the shadows and literally have us for dinner. So we waited, with darkness approaching fast.

The rain stopped as fast as it had come. As always, there is bad news and good news in these types of situations. The bad was that we were stuck in the mud.

But the good news was that we were now all witnesses to a double rainbow over the Serengeti. Clear, colorful and beautiful. These two magnificent arches of color had us giggling like school kids. Especially the guys.

The weird part. This was not the rainy season. That's why the guide was caught off guard when the rain came in so fast. Yet here we were. Rhinos, rain and rainbows!

So let's recap what had happened so far. Our group of four adventurers stayed focused on our goal. We were in Africa to fully experience Africa. We said "yes" to the possibility that the final safari might be memorable.

We did not choose comfort over effort. We did not give in to being too tired to see our trip through to the very end. I would say our decision and our effort was paying off. Wouldn't you?

We enjoyed the rare sighting of two black rhinoceros, experienced seldom-seen rain on the Serengeti, and then there was the beauty of a double rainbow. How crazy cool was that?

Yes, there were some struggles and a few scary moments. Such is life. Getting through those moments adds to the richness of life. We grow stronger because of them. They enrich our stories, lessons and memories.

You talk about stories to tell . . . Plus, we had pictures to prove it. Lots of pictures! We were all laughing about the people back at camp who were missing out. How stupid they were for doing ordinary things when we were having an extraordinary experience.

But that's what average people do. They think average thoughts, take average actions and have average results. They pack clothes. They are thinking about tomorrow while forgetting about today.

Back to the adventure. Now we were beginning to get worried. Darkness was coming fast and we were still stuck. Darkness means two things. Tough to see and the wildlife would be coming out to have their dinner. We didn't want to be the main course!

It took almost fifteen minutes of rocking back and forth before the vehicle broke loose of the muddy surface. We were off, driving fast to try to stay on top of the silky, muddy surface. We were slipping and sliding toward the pretend road.

Because the various safari vehicles drove the makeshift road every day, its packed surface would support our vehicle and get us back to camp safely.

But wait . . . there's more! Our vehicle had been racing darkness, when our guide began to slow down. We were within ten minutes of our camp. We all stopped laughing. Now what? What could possibly be going on now?

Between the raindrops left on our vehicle's rain-soaked side curtains, we peeked out. There they were. A massive herd of elephants was crossing the road right in front of our vehicle.

Huge bull elephants, mamma elephants, and tiny babies lumbered along. Young and very old were in the mix. Our guide explained that in the bush, wildlife has the right-of-way.

Once the herd reached the other side of the road, they began lying down and rolling around in the puddles of the water-soaked land. Because rain is so scarce, when it happens, all the animals come out to play. It was a thrilling and amazing sight to see.

I wanted to get out of the vehicle so bad . . . It looked like such fun to just roll around in the muddy mess. If elephants could laugh, I know they would have. The biggest and the smallest were all taking time to enjoy the moment.

To this day I would swear that one of the baby elephants winked at me with a big beautiful joyful eye. It was as if she was saying, "Don't forget to take time to be playful."

I got the message loud and clear. There had been a lot of long hard days, months and years in my life. There still would be. But now I would be sure to add much more play and playfulness into the mix.

Our group was lucky. We enjoyed a few moments of immense pleasure with these magnificent beasts. And then it was back to camp.

We had stories to tell and pictures to share. We had grown closer because of the shared experience. We felt happy, satisfied and complete, We saw our goal through to the end. Our reward had been an extraordinary experience full of many lasting memories!

SEEING IT THROUGH

As you answer the following questions, think about your professional life and then your personal life. Don't answer the questions the way you think you should answer them. That would be useless and a complete waste of time.

Be completely honest. Your answers are key in discovering areas where you can make changes and enjoy even greater success.

What would you do? Would you stay at camp to pack luggage? Choose comfort over effort? Or take a chance by going on an adventure?

When have you done the easy thing, when you know you could have put in extra effort? What were the results?

What happened the last time you almost reached a goal? Did you stop, give in, give up or become too tired to finish? Or maybe you pushed through and did whatever it took to reach your goal.

How could including play and being more playful improve your professional and personal goals? What specifically will you do to be more playful? What's your plan?

Within our group, we all had a goal. Some people let packing luggage get in the way of seeing their goal through to the very end. They became distracted, lazy and lost out because of their choice.

When we lose focus or let the wrong things get in our way, we miss out on opportunities and possibilities. We can miss what matters most.

SATISFACTION, AT LAST

Don't give up or give in. This is an opportunity to complete a goal and enjoy the satisfaction that goes with finishing what you've started.

1. Name a goal where you stopped short and did not follow through to the end.

2. Name a goal where you chose comfort over effort and then fell short of completing the goal.

3. Choose the goal you want to focus on and finish first.

   Why is it important for you to complete this goal?

   What, specifically, will you do to ensure your success?

   What is your action plan?

   When will you complete the goal?

Once you complete your goal – how will you CELEBRATE?

Good job!

Execution is the point of separation!

Now, read Chapter Seven.

CHAPTER SEVEN

It's Called Execution
for a Reason

THE POINT OF SEPARATION

Execution separates those who talk about making it big and those who do what it takes to actually make it happen.

It is imperative that you remain committed to getting what you want and stay laser-focused on execution. Consistency in execution will accelerate your growth and your achievements. It will catapult you past your competition.

UP TO YOU, BABY!

You achieve killer results when you focus on the execution. Goals without execution disappear, while killing your hopes, dreams and aspirations.

When a goal is not met, feelings of being overwhelmed, fear, anger, frustration and disappointment take over. Emotions are dialed up, and performance is dialed down or extinguished.

No matter how good the plan is or how carefully the steps are laid out, without execution, it all falls apart. Either way, it's all up to YOU, baby!

> *I definitely felt like I had a Secret Weapon.*
> *What Deborah taught me is legit!*
> — *James, NFL wide receiver*

THIS SHIT IS LEGIT!

Ever since he was a little boy, James had dreams of making it into the NFL. Although he didn't make the draft, he had an opportunity to show off his skills to the NFL teams during an upcoming pro day. Everything was on the line.

His agent called and told me that James, a wide receiver, needed to run the forty-yard dash at a speed of 4.40 seconds before the scouts would take a serious look at him.

Both James and his agent understood the extreme pressure of this one event. They knew that if James couldn't execute, all of his hopes and dreams would disappear.

When James and I began meeting, our focus was strictly on execution. What, exactly and specifically, would it take for James to perform at his ultimate best while under extreme pressure?

Learning to stay calm, confident and focused was imperative. He needed to explode off the line and run past the finish line. If James focused on the actual finish line, his mind would be fooled into thinking he was done. His speed would slow. Even milliseconds were imperative to his success.

We focused on two things: how James would create his ultimate state of performance and how he would remain calm and confident standing in line waiting for his turn to run.

Watching other players perform while standing in line waiting for his turn could prove to be excruciating. James knew his competitors would be jumping up and down in line as they tried to calm their nerves. This just added to the intensity of the situation.

This was not an option for James. Seems like a small thing, but it wasn't. All that additional movement would burn up energy that James would need to burst off the line and then finish fast. Every aspect of a perfect execution was broken down.

James learned calming techniques that could be used in the moment and on demand. He could save his energy, remain resilient and focused.

Then he learned E-magination™ (imagining with emotion), a technique whereby he deeply imagined his perfect performance. We tricked his brain into experiencing success before it actually happened. He now knew what his perfect state of performance looked and felt like. He was ready.

With his confidence raised, along with his trust in his ability to perform, James felt prepared. He had increased his odds for success. He was prepared to execute every aspect of his performance.

At 6:00 AM on his pro day, I received a call from James. He was excited and grateful. It was show time, and he believed in himself.

Four hours later, my cellphone chirped and I saw a text message from James's agent. It read, "James just ran a 4.32! The scouts are talking to him now!"

I ran around my house screaming like a little kid. This was huge. Reading and re-reading the text message, I knew a young man's lifelong dreams had been in the balance. His discipline, hard work and amazing talent had been recognized. His life was about to change forever.

By focusing on the specifics of the execution, the results took care of themselves.

A few months later, James was in an NFL uniform at training camp, practicing next to his football idols. He made it because he put his focus on the execution. The results, he achieved his ultimate goal!

WINNING IS FOR LOSERS

What is winning for you? Closing the sale, being awarded the contract, getting up on stage and remembering your speech, having the lowest score or the highest score?

Whatever winning is for you, stop focusing on the win. Winning is a goal. It's a destination. When people are focused on winning, they lose sight of the individual ingredients that it takes to win. The key to performance is to focus on the individual effort and execution.

I'm not saying to forget about goals. You always need something to "bump up against." Goals, statistics and quotas let us know how well we are doing with the execution.

But here's the thing to remember: a sales professional focused on his or her quota instead of the specific steps necessary to execute every aspect of a sale will have a very puny commission check. The result of that is lost confidence, frustration and worry.

James and his agent knew that 4.40 seconds was the goal. That was realistic. They were excited about potentials and possibilities. They also understood the importance of staying focused on execution.

James did the work necessary to prepare for this life-altering event. He knew that his talent, knowledge and experience were not going to be enough to get him to that next level.

He needed to learn how to count on himself. James learned how to be clear, calm and confident under extreme pressure. And he knew how to turn up the heat when he needed it most.

James went from setting realistic goals to achieving idealistic results. You can do the same.

YOU ARE THE EDGE

After moving to Phoenix, my goals were simple. Get out of the house, not talk baby talk and make enough money to put my youngest into a really good preschool. That was it!

Owning a corporation was not on my radar. It wasn't on some vision board or on a list of goals. Neither was coaching and training business professionals and professional athletes.

From the beginning, my focus has remained on execution. All of my studies of neuroscience, brain research, human behavior, stress reduction and all the rest were to ensure I always had an edge.

That edge was me. I managed the bold and the subtle aspects of how I performed. Execution was up to me.

James focused on his execution so he could achieve extraordinary results. He managed what he would do, when he would do it, how he would do it and to what degree.

He knew exactly what to think, how to feel and what to believe to create his ultimate state of high performance.

James WAS the Edge he was searching for and found!

CREATE YOUR CLEAR EDGE

Be specific with all of your answers to the following.

When you are at your ultimate best . . .

- What are you thinking? Your specific thoughts.

- What feelings do you experience? Name them.

- How do you behave / act / perform?

- What do you believe about yourself, your talent, your knowledge and your skills?

- Remember a time in the past when you were at your best. Describe it.

The answer to these questions is your
Ultimate State of High Performance!

CHAPTER EIGHT

Fit In
and Fail

The strength of the team is each
individual member. The strength of
each member is the team.

– Phil Jackson

NO "I" IN TEAM ... RIDICULOUS

The concept of *No "I" in TEAM* is ridiculous. Taking the "I" out of team is a waste of time, money, creativity and individuality. The focus has to be on the "I" first and the team second. Teams are made up of individuals. If you lose the "I", who is going to do the work?

Focusing on the team first sucks. It sucks the lifeblood, the motivation, and the uniqueness out of each individual member of the team. It's true for businesses, organization, groups or a team of athletes.

It's imperative that each individual bring to the team his or her most creative ideas, excitement and desire to get the job done and done well. That's called progress, change, upping the game and beating the competition!

FITTING IN IS FAILING

Fitting in is failing. It's not fun. It's not rewarding. It is a cop-out. If the goal is to fit in, then you've failed. You fail at being you. You fail at getting your ideas heard. You fail at taking the necessary actions that will propel you into greatness.

That's not all. When someone fits in, he or she fails the team, too. The team deserves everybody's best. If the goal is for the team to win, and it should be, then each individual must do his or her job and do it extremely well.

When high achievers attempt to fit in, blend in, and be part of a group, they can go numb and dumb. It's painful and upsetting … especially if you are the one who is dumbing down and numbing out.

Top performers feel a sense of urgency when faced with a challenge. They are excited. They are preparing to go after the challenge. Numbing out and dumbing down goes against their personality.

If a team member asks the question, "What do you think we should do?" and the top performer answers, "Whatever the rest of you want to do is fine with me," then that person is numbing out and dumbing down.

They are not saying what they really think. They give up on their personal point of view. They stop sharing their ideas. Others take control of the results. Stress begins to build up, and so will resentment. Going numb and dumb is not a plan for success.

DON'T PUT YOURSELF ON THE BENCH

This is not the time to lay low and play dumb. You are smart, creative and have ideas—don't hold back. When you have an opportunity to head to the front of the room, take your seat at the head of the table or be that breakout star during a game— do it!

Too many times I have heard, "But Deborah, I don't want to make other people feel bad!" Are you kidding me? No one can be held responsible for how other people feel.

People often feel bad when others are succeeding. They feel bad because they don't have the guts to do it themselves. They would rather point fingers at someone else than at themselves. Not your problem.

This is not a time to go pout and sit on the bench. This is the time to play your best game ever.

GAME ON!

When another potential superstar sees you pushing the limits, going outside the boundaries and succeeding, what is he or she going to do?

I'll tell you what that person should do. What real professionals do. What competitive performers do. They do whatever he or she can do to top you. Not stop you; top you. That's competing at a high level.

When done right, you praise each other. You both feed off the excitement of a hard-fought challenge. You challenge each other to do more, be more and succeed more. It's game on!

You both win, and so does the team. Sometimes it just takes one person to take a risk. It gives other people on the team "permission" to excel too.

If they step up, great. If they don't, it's not your problem. You don't need to fix them. Focus on you! Execute. It's all up to you, baby!

YOU FIRST

As always, don't judge what your write. Act like an investigator. Follow the clues and get to the facts.

Make an assessment and then take action!

1. Identify where you are fitting in and blending in.

2. Where have you been behaving numb and dumb?

3. What are you going to do about it? How exactly will you push past self-imposed limitations?

4. When and where will you make your move? Be specific!

THE
GAME CHANGER

Fear is King . . . until you master it.
                                    — Deborah Dubree

TAME & TRAIN YOUR B.E.A.S.T.™

This section is a game changer. It is the key to execution. It IS the competitive edge high performers seek.

This is the difference between those who hide out and shrink back at that moment right before they get what they really want and those who make bold decisions and take the ballsy action necessary to accelerate into high performance. The ones who go after and get what they want most.

The Tame & Train Your B.E.A.S.T.™ method is not cutesy or cuddly. I am not going to coddle you when it comes to this. It's too important to your success. It works!

Some people may think they are too macho or special for a method that includes emotions. It sounds soft or mushy. That's the exact type of thinking that keeps people from getting to the top and staying there.

This method is the exact same one I use when coaching and training executives, sales professionals, entrepreneurs, NFL players, pro golfers and student-athletes who all want to perform at their ultimate best.

They all want to get noticed, make a lot more money and earn the respect they deserve. They are all looking for that competitive edge that sets them apart from their competition. This is the answer they've been seeking.

Miss This And Continue To Struggle To Succeed

When I started studying and applying the methods I'm going to share in this section, every challenge I met and opportunity I jumped at became easier to face and achieve. It differentiated me from the rest.

As a disclaimer, I clearly state that I do not have a magic wand. Sorry! I know how disappointing that may be to some. But no one does. Struggles still happen. Fear still occurs. So what!

It is not, and has never been, about the fear. It's not about the frustration, stress, anger, being overwhelmed or all the rest. It comes down to how long people are willing to struggle, worry and wait while opportunities pass them by. It's a timing issue.

How much time will pass, after an error, before they get their head out of their crack and back into the game fast?

How long before they grow the courage to make that bold decision, stay committed to getting what they want and take the ballsy action necessary to make it happen? It all leads to action! Focus on what matters instead of continuing to waste money, time and energy on a bunch of BS.

Your level of play is determined by how well you Tame & Train The B.E.A.S.T.

Everyone faces the BEAST. You can deny it, try to ignore it or attempt to push it aside. You will lose. The BEAST will win … every time.

The BEAST is sneaky. It's mean. It's vindictive. It's resentful. It does not give a crap about how pretty you are, smart you are or intelligent you are. It could care less about the size of your bank account or the plushness of your office. It just doesn't care!

And, it loves to bully you, scare you and beat the crap out of you when you are most vulnerable. It will embarrass you and overwhelm you right when you are about to face the most critical decision or the most important performance of your life.

You cannot control it. If anyone tells you that you can, they are wrong. You can tame it. You can train it. It cannot be controlled.

TAME and TRAIN

Over the next five chapters, you will discover the most misunderstood, underutilized and powerful aspect of being a high performance player.

When the BEAST is tamed and trained, your courage, power, confidence and clarity are at an all-time high. You develop a bit of a swagger. People begin to notice you. You are focused on what's most important. You win!

THE B.E.A.S.T.

B	Beliefs	Don't Believe Your Own BS
E	Emotions	Pick and Choose Your Emotions
A	Acute Awareness	6 "A"s of Acute Awareness
S	SELF-Identity	You Matter To You
T	Talk and Walk	Win–Win Combination

CHAPTER NINE

Don't Believe
Your Own BS

Whether your sunglasses are off or on,
you only see the world you make.

— Bonnie Raitt

It's up to each individual to figure out what is true and not true when it comes to his or her beliefs. If you buy into your own bullshit beliefs, than you will also pay the crappy consequences. It's a package deal. Pretty cut and dry. Like these examples.

- A speaker believes she is supposed to be nervous every time she goes on stage. So she experiences the jitters—upset-stomach, heart-pounding and palms-sweating pre-speech stress.

  She ends up forgetting parts of her speech, stammering and stuttering to remember what to say next. She loses the respect of her audience, along with future opportunities and business connections.

- Athletes who believe that they've lost their touch will

go into a slump. They disappoint themselves and their team. Big contract deals disappear. So does their self-respect.

- You believe the person across the conference table is a better negotiator than you are. So you back off or back down when pushed. Sales go down and profits disappear. Maybe your job, too.

- Children who believe in Santa Claus behave in a way that supports their belief. Especially in the month of December. Tell a child that Santa won't bring presents if he or she misbehaves and the child stops crying, shares a toy and stops pulling on the dog's ear—because the child believes.

TRUTH and CONSEQUENCES

Smart and talented people do really stupid stuff based on their unfounded, untrue and unreliable beliefs. Beliefs about themselves, about others, about situations and events, as well as beliefs about inanimate objects.

Here is the scary part. Beliefs are not always true. And you act according to what you believe! So really get this. Not everything you believe is true. True or not, you will act according to what you believe. The actions you take or don't take will cause results. The results have consequences.

Who do you think gets to deal with the consequences? Tag, you're it!

BAD CLUB! BAD CLUB!

When Jim called, he was leaving in a month to travel to Ireland for a huge, internationally televised golf event. He is a highly competitive pro golfer, and he knew that the golf course he would be competing on would be a tough one.

It would demand the use of his three-wood. Considering it the worst club in his bag, Jim would do anything to keep from having to use it. He hated that club.

Performing well at this prestigious event was imperative. Jim had a lot at risk. He could lose money, the respect of his peers and invitations to future career-building golfing opportunities. He had to learn to trust himself, that club and his ability to use that club to play solid golf.

During our first day together at the driving range, Jim's pro golf instructor joined us. After polite introductions, I demanded to see "THE" club. Hesitantly, Jim handed it to me.

I rolled the club around in my hand for a couple of moments. Then I vigorously began shaking my pointer finger at the club and reprimanded it, "Bad club! Bad club!"

I thought the guys were going to bust a gut laughing. They knew exactly what I meant. The non-thinking, non-breathing club was not the problem. It was time to face the truth. The club was only responding to the person swinging it.

Jim, on the other hand, was acting according to what he believed was true. He believed that the club was the problem. It was much easier to believe that than to blame himself.

Because he felt the club was the problem, he started changing his technique to match the problem he was having with the club. When he changed his technique, it threw off the rest of his game. (Sound familiar, Tiger?)

We addressed the core problem. Not Jim; not the club. We address the belief. The belief wasn't good or bad—it was simply a belief. But the belief created bad consequences. It needed to be changed!

Jim and I discussed what he would have to believe to play at his absolute best. He remembered all the great shots he had made over his career. He stopped blaming the club and started believing in himself, his talent and his skills.

Jim took back his control. He made a conscious choice about what he would believe, instead of allowing the belief to control his thinking, his behavior and the results of that behavior. Once the belief was changed, Jim and the club could 'play nice' again!

Jim adjusted his pre-shot routine to include his belief in himself and his trust in his ability to be powerful and accurate with the three-wood. Jim quickly went back to playing highly competitive golf. His skill and talent were never in question. Now, with a new belief, Jim started getting the results he wanted.

Jim won a big share of the purse, enjoyed a free trip to Ireland and was offered an exemption into a prestigious PGA tournament. His television appearance boosted his career, and he definitely earned the respect of his peers. He was a winner on multiple levels.

BELIEVE and ACHIEVE IS A MYTH

Believe and you will achieve is what many experts preach. Good luck with that. It's a myth!

Here are three important factors about beliefs that I discovered over the years. People like to say they believe in something when what they really mean is, "I'm thinking about it."

"I believe I could be the next superstar, top sales person, million dollar speaker, extraordinary leader, etc." These are superficial words that have little or no meaning.

Just because someone uses the word believe or belief in a sentence doesn't make it true. What they are really doing is trying to talk themselves into actually believing their own words. They are thinking it over and pondering the possibility of believing.

Beliefs are deep, ingrained and cannot be ignored. Beliefs are powerful. No one can talk you out of your belief. It belongs to you and you alone. Beliefs are motivational. They encourage confidence and push you into action.

My second discovery is this. Unless you have developed the ability to go up to a mountain top, sit down, cross your legs, begin to hum and have things drop out of the sky – you have to put effort and execution into making your beliefs come true.

Remember execution? The formula for success is: believe, execute with consistency and achieve.

The third discovery is that beliefs need to be examined. Ask yourself, "What's true or not true about this belief?" Based on the answer, either change the untrue belief into a belief that is true. Or reinforce and leverage the belief to gain greater motivation, power and influence over your actions.

You get to choose what you don't believe in and what you do believe in. Choose carefully. Consider these beliefs.

Las Vegas is alive and very wealthy because people believe that the next pull of the handle or the next roll of the dice will win them huge payoffs.

Parents watch their children in dance, sports, school and various other activities, believing that their child is The One. The one who is more talented and more special than all other children. What their children believe matters more.

Every week in sports, we see players who hold onto hope

and make a winning surge in the fourth quarter, with the clock ticking down and fans that are leaving the stands. Beliefs help overcome the odds.

I believe in beliefs that are believed in. Ponder that for a moment. What you believe matters. It matters to you and to your career, relationships, legacy, finances and health. Your success or failure in each of these areas can be directly linked to what you believe to be true and the actions you take because of those beliefs.

When I had a full knee replacement, I asked my surgeon how long my recovery would be. He stated the rehabilitation process typically meant using a walker and then switching to using a cane. I could plan on the process taking eight weeks after surgery. I did it in three weeks. I believed in me, not statistics.

An NFL client injured his arm during a game. He tore the triceps eighty percent. We began setting both realistic and idealist goals all throughout his rehabilitation.

With his doctor's approval to proceed and the player's unwavering belief in himself, he consistently pushed his trainer to add weights to his routine. His progress was remarkable. Week after week, he met the idealistic goals. He finished rehabilitation two months earlier that he expected. He believed in himself over the standards that had been set by others. It took effort and execution.

Entrepreneurs continue to try to beat the odds by simply believing in themselves, their ideas, their products and their services. It is not a sustainable model for success.

The entrepreneurs and business professionals who become successful and earn millions are the ones who are willing to do whatever it takes to overcome limitations and circumstances that would cause others to throw in the towel and give up. They understand the formula. They believe, they execute consistently and they achieve.

In each of these examples, the person believed in himself or herself. They believed in the possibility of reaching their goal. Then, each executed according to his or her belief. Each took the necessary action to achieve more than what seemed reasonable or possible to others. Don't worry about what others believe. Their beliefs don't matter.

It's imperative to know what you believe. Leverage the beliefs that work in your favor. Cut the crap that doesn't. If you don't pay attention and consciously choose what you believe, the beliefs will choose you. You may be highly disappointed by their choice.

FIVE TRUTHS ABOUT BELIEFS

1. Beliefs are sneaky. They lurk around in the shadows of our mind.

   Cell biologist Bruce Lipton, PhD, author of *The Biology of Belief: Unleashing the Power of Consciousness, Matter, and Miracles* shares that 95% to 99% of the time, we are not even aware of our beliefs and our behaviors.

   Now that's what I would call numb and dumb!

2. Beliefs are extremely powerful. They can cause the strongest to buckle at the knees. They have smart people doing and saying really stupid stuff.

3. Beliefs are not always true. It's up to you to determine what is true for you.

4. Some beliefs were true in the past, but not true anymore.

5. True or not, you act/perform/behave according to your beliefs.

CUT THE CRAP

It is time for *Truth and Consequences*. Whatever a person believes to be true, whether it is true or not, that person is the one who experiences the full weight of the consequences.

Take action to cut the crap and stop buying into your own BS.

1. What excuses do you repeatedly tell yourself or others? Examples: I'm too old, short, tall or fat to ____. Not smart enough to _____. Not good at _____ .

2. What do you worry about?

3. What have authority figures told you in the past, that you accepted as true, but are not true?

4. What has society repeatedly stated as being the truth, but it is not YOUR truth?

5. Review your answers about your beliefs? What empowering beliefs do you have? How can you leverage them?

6. What beliefs do you want to cut and replace? What is the empowering replacement belief?

ACTION PLAN: How will you act, behave, execute differently based on your new beliefs?

CHAPTER TEN

Pick and Choose Emotions

EMOTIONS ARE FOR SISSIES

Emotions are for sissies. They make you weak. There is no room in business for emotions.

During my twenty-five years in the world of construction, the common and quite strong opinion was that emotions don't belong in business. They definitely make you weak. They are unacceptable.

> *In my opinion, that is the most ridiculous, unfounded and idiotic statement I've ever heard. What idiot would spew such nonsense? Are you kidding me! I'll bet they also think that the world is flat and that pigs can fly!*

Oh wait . . . sorry, that was a bit emotional, wasn't it?

Emotions exist throughout business, sports, relationships, home, parenting and recreation. We are human. We are emotional. Accept it! And learn to use emotions to your benefit.

Every sale that is made or lost is emotionally based. Every decision made is emotionally based. Every negotiation is won or lost based on who managed their emotions best.

NEGOTIATIONS 101

He had some of the sweetest and smoothest moves I have ever witnessed. Watching Kevin close sales on multimillion-dollar contracts with such ease was truly an art form.

This was the day. It was early in my career and I was excited to learn about negotiations from an expert. Contractors were set to arrive at our office at their appointed time to negotiate the finer points of each of their contracts. Once agreed upon, we could sign the deal and get started building the new project.

My role was simple—watch and learn. The experience had tremendous impact. What I learned continues to benefit me even today. Back in the early days, just being in the emotionally charged room while negotiations were taking place made me nervous.

One by one, the various contractors showed up at our office. As each one entered our conference room, I began to notice their subtle signs of nervousness.

One had trouble just choosing which chair to sit in. He seemed to be looking for the one that possessed the magical power position.

One could barely look Kevin in the eyes as they bantered back and forth. It felt like I was on a tilt-a-whirl with another, as he twisted and turned in his swivel chair.

There was a vast array of throat-clearing, nervous ticks, sweaty hands, legs bouncing and voices stammering.

During a break between meetings, Kevin explained to me, "I know the minute they walk into the room if I have the upper hand. Any show of nervousness gives me the edge."

Watching more closely, I began to see how right he was. There were many times when Kevin would just stop and say nothing. The silence was almost unbearable. His edge increased as the other person became stressed, not knowing what to say or do.

Because of our previous discussions, I knew there were specific points at which Kevin could have easily let the contractor win. His goal was always to be fair, but also to come out ahead.

A vast majority of the contractors were off their game. They would back down or give in when they could have just as easily held their ground and pushed for better terms.

They kissed money good-bye, simply because emotional stress got the best of them and muddled their thinking.

Kevin managed his emotions. He actually had fun and was excited by the experience. Not only did he negotiate well, but he also picked up money and often better terms on each contract.

The bottom line is simple. Manage emotions and you win. If emotions control you, you lose. A lot!

NEGOTIATION IS EVERYWHERE

Have you ever been in a negotiation and the other person insulted you? Then you got mad or upset. Do you understand that at that very moment, the other person won? He or she just got the upper hand.

Maybe the other person strategically did something to tick you off, or maybe he or she just stumbled onto something that upset you. Either way, that person moved into the position of power. You are now caught in a position of defending yourself and your point of view. That's a weak spot to be in.

What about the negotiations you conduct with your kids? Have your kids ever ticked you off? Have they made you so mad that they won the battle? You gave in or gave up out of frustration. Maybe you walked out of the room or sent them to their room, because you needed to settle down.

Has that same scenario ever happened with a love relationship? Negotiations are in every aspect of your life. Think about shopping for furniture, a car or a house. Have you ever lost control of your emotions, becoming frustrated, upset or angry? Then walked away or lost out on getting what you wanted?

Knowing how to manage your emotions is imperative to winning at negotiations in every part of your life.

MONEY and EMOTIONS DO NOT MIX

Stockbrokers deeply understand the power of emotions. They are very smart and very analytical. They invest huge amounts of time and money developing an exact plan around their investing strategies.

The plan will lay out exactly when they will jump in and when they will jump out of the market. They know their tolerance numbers.

Even the best plans did not take human emotions into account. By the time I was called the stockbrokers were losing money or not making as much money as they could. They were frustrated, worried and upset. They would jump in or out of the market too quickly. Their emotions were screwing up their well developed plan. They were losing money, time and their patience.

Once they learned how to manage their emotional rollercoaster under the extreme pressure of the constantly changing market, they were able to manage their portfolios with greater results. It took getting a grip on their emotions before their talents and intelligence could kick back in.

GET A GRIP

Emotions That Weaken: *anger; fear; frustration; anxiety; hopelessness; resentment; worry; concern; sadness; agony; being overwhelmed; guilt; unworthiness; shame; blame; panic; remorse; and many more.*

You can try to ignore them, deny them, shove them down and forget them . . . but emotions are always there. They will not go away or be ignored.

Whether you're going onstage for a critical speech, meeting with that million-dollar client, negotiating your next business contract or presenting ideas to the board of directors—you can't afford to get stressed out, look stupid, lose respect or lose sales. Get a grip!

DANGER – DANGER

Anyone who tells you that you can control your emotions is an idiot. Emotions can't be controlled. They just happen and they happen in nanoseconds. The good news is that you can manage them. Notice them first and then manage them.

According to Web MD®, seventy-five percent to ninety percent of all doctor's office visits are for stress-related ailments and complaints.

Stressful emotions like anger, fear, frustration, anxiety and even sadness weaken the body and the mind. They affect your personal and professional bottom line.

What happens to your income if you get sick? How many

times a day or week or month do you suffer from backaches, shoulder stiffness, headaches and upset stomach? Have any trouble getting a good night's sleep? Ever lash out at people or lash in at yourself?

All are signs of stress. They will all disrupt or disable your ability to perform. They take you out and shut you down. Money is lost. People are disappointed. Health is compromised.

> *Stress could easily become our next public health crisis.*
> **– American Psychological Association CEO Norman Anderson**

THE MANY FACES OF STRESS

Here are some situations and emotional triggers that cause stress.

- Anything new or different; the mind considers it a threat and triggers the stress emotions.

- Anything you don't understand.

- Messing up; making a mistake will lead to feeling humiliated, ashamed, sad, disappointed and overwhelmed.

- Pressure of expectations; your own expectations or the expectations of others.

- Fear of disappointing family, friends, peers, bosses, agents, coaches and yourself.

- Watching others fail and hoping that it doesn't happen to you.

- Seeking approval … and not getting it.
- Watching others succeed and wondering, "Am I good enough?"
- Being around others who are nervous, angry or frustrated.
- Getting yelled at or anticipating you might get yelled at.
- The pressure of knowing this is a *"make it or break it"* situation.

CRASH and BURN

When under stress, people literally can't think clearly. Their mind fogs up and logic is lost. Ever hear someone say, "Leave me alone; I can't think straight right now"? They are right. They can't.

Emotional stress causes really smart people to do and say really stupid stuff. Their mind shuts down. They hesitate to make a decision. Deals are lost.

Or they act too quickly, out of desperation. They make a bad decision that can be very costly. It's all about emotions.

People who love each other will scream and holler at each other during a disagreement, because they have not been taught how to manage their emotions. Or they might shut down completely, go into hibernation and shut the other person out.

Unmanaged emotions cause the body to go weak. It causes the muscles to tense up, and flexibility is reduced. Response time is slower. Plus, the heart pounds, the palms sweat and the stomach churns.

Kiss any hope of performing well, much less preforming at your ultimate best, good-bye. You will crash and burn.

EMOTIONS CAN BE YOUR BEST FRIEND

Emotions That Empower: *love; gratitude; appreciation; joy; happiness; confidence; calm; contentment; passion; excitement; being fired up, thrilled, cheerful, pleased, relaxed and many more.*

Emotions can be your best friend. They can help push you beyond your own expectations. They motivate you, pump you up and can give you a swift kick in the butt.

Old-school thinking was that emotions like these weaken you. That kind of thinking is wrong. In fact, just the opposite is true. Physiologically, they strengthen you.

Think about it this way. You can get all mushy and love someone, look them in the eyes and whisper sweet words in their ear. That's one level of love. Great for loving relationships. Not recommended for business.

Have you ever watched 300-pound football players doing a victory dance in the end zone, as they pat each other on the butt and knock helmets? That's love as well. Love of the game. Love for their team members. Love for the score they just made. It's simply a different level and application of the same emotion. It strengthens the player, motivates them to do more and to do even better. The level of energy is just as strong, but applied differently.

You can love to negotiate and be excited by it, like Kevin. It is powerful and definitely belongs in business. You will feel more confident and think more clearly. Choosing the right emotions to fit the situation is the key. And you have to stay conscious to do that.

Emotions will power you up or take you down. You get to

choose. The best way to empower yourself emotionally is to get really clear on what emotions push you to be at your best in any situation.

MAKE IT FIT

Emotions need to fit the situation. Not all emotions are created equal. If you are sitting in a boardroom negotiating a contract, you want to feel clear, calm, in control and confident.

At home with your family, you may want to feel loving, kind, caring and giving. On a ski run, the feelings that best fit the situation may be dominant, engaged, powerful, confident and focused.

Always know what emotions are exactly right for you, in any situation. The key to high performance is to know and manage your emotions. To do this takes planning ahead.

MANAGING EMOTIONS

Emotions That Weaken: *anger; fear; frustration; anxiety; hopelessness; resentment; worry; concern; sadness; agony; being overwhelmed; guilt; unworthiness; shame; blame; panic; remorse; and many more.*

You can manage emotion when you are aware.

First, what are your current DEFAULT emotions? These are your 'go to' emotions that show up when you are stressed out.

1. What stresses you out? Get specific. Think about your career, health, self-image, finances, relationships and more.

2. What are your default emotions? The ones you go to most often when you are under stress? Use the list above of Emotions That Weaken as a guide.

Emotions That Empower: *love; gratitude; appreciation; joy; happiness; confidence; calm; contentment; passion; excitement; being fired up, thrilled, cheerful, pleased, relaxed and many more.*

3. What emotions empower you? Drive you to perform at your ultimate best? Use the Emotions That Empower list above as a guide.

4. Now, revisit your default emotions in #2. Replace those emotions that weaken you with emotions that empower you. Remember, each emotion has multiple applications and levels.

Make a plan: What will be different the next time you are faced with the stressors you listed in question #1?

How will you apply your answers in question #4, so you get a different outcome and result?

CHAPTER ELEVEN

6 "A"s to
Acute Awareness

It always amazes me how many people don't wake up before they come to work. They are not aware of what's going on and they really don't seem to care.

Once a week I'll answer my phone by saying, "Hello, this is Deborah."

The person on the other end of the phone line asks, "Is Deborah there?" Are you kidding me? I just said my name! The next thing the caller hears is "click"!

Unbelievable. People are on autopilot. They lack focus. They just don't care. They are simply going through the motions.

Successful top performers plan for results. They expect successful results. They make sure the odds are in their favor. Then they execute. You must stay awake and aware.

ALL ABOUT ME!

Being acutely aware of yourself, others, your environment, the results you want to achieve and the situation you are in are all imperative to growth and success.

Setting myself apart from the crowd continues to be a focus of mine. I learned early in my career the benefit of having an "All About Me Plan" for any type of meeting, event or situation. It helped me stay focused on results and how best to achieve them.

I used this strategy and planning process for any type of meeting or encounter. It could be casual or formal. It might include other contractors, my peers, my staff or outside bankers and lawyers. It might be a one-to-one meeting or a large group.

This "All About Me Plan" could be for an organizational meeting or networking event. The elements of the plan are always similar. They might expand or contract, based on the actual meeting. Following are some of the elements and questions to consider in developing your own "All About Me Plan."

Ask yourself the following before your next encounter: *What end result do I want to achieve by the time I walk out of the meeting? Who else will be in the room?*

Who do "I" want to be in the room? Is it more advantageous for me to be a person of authority, a listener, or a contributor? How do I want the other people in the room to feel . . . about the meeting, about me, about my company?

Considering the end result I want to achieve: *Where will I sit? Who will I sit next to or across from? What will I wear? When will I show up? What do I need to bring to the meeting to strengthen my point and position?*

What specific questions do I want to ask? Who do I want to answer the questions? Who might I want to impress or impact? How exactly will I ensure that I impress or impact the person or situation?

During the meeting, you might not say a word. Your goal is to observe, listen and learn. Or, you may dominate the conversation. You might ask a question and then sit back and observe who takes the ball and runs with it.

Sometimes you can back up someone else's point of view,

which you also believe in. This increases your rapport, along with empowering a joint effort.

Being acutely aware before, during and after meetings is critical to success. As an ultimate observer, you quickly learn what works and doesn't work with certain people and in specific situations. You can then adjust before the next encounter.

DANGEROUS DISTRACTIONS

Has something like this ever happened to you?

You are in the middle of preparing a critical report for an upcoming meeting and your email dings. You start to read the most "who gives a crap" email, and then you overhear laughter in the break room. So you get up to go see what's going on. You get to the break room and get involved in a conversation with a bunch of non-productive people. The alarm on your phone goes off, reminding you of the very important meeting you're attending in fifteen minutes. You go running back to your office, knowing you're screwed because the critical document you were preparing for the meeting is not done! Panic sets in. There is no time to recover. You are about to look like an idiot in front of your peers and your client.

Sound way too familiar? The inability to get focused and stay focused is costly. Distractions by non-important or less important stuff can steal your attention before you even know it's happening. The results can be painful, upsetting, costly and even dangerous.

In baseball, if a batter loses focus, he or she could strike out or get hit by the ball. Either way, it hurts.

An entrepreneur can lose focus of what's most important to their business and find that they are off working on little tasks that have nothing to do with bringing in clients and closing sales. Next thing they know, he or she is out of business and has become a statistic.

A business professional that becomes distracted will miss deadlines, details and the needs of their clients. They lose clients. They lose self-respect and their reputation. And they could also lose their job.

Lose focus when driving, and the next sounds you will hear are crushing metal, police sirens and the four-letter rants of angry drivers.

INQUIRING MINDS WANT TO KNOW

Gaining and keeping focus requires an understanding of how your brain operates and what to do to make it to work for you.

Our mind is like a little kid. It is constantly losing focus. It goes off in any and all directions, searching for shiny objects and things to keep it entertained.

It also searches the environment for potential danger. It's a smart and busy brain, just not well directed. It's your job to give it direction.

The best way to snap it back to attention is to ask it questions. The brain is a problem-solving machine. By asking the right questions, you keep it focused on getting results. By focusing on results, you also eliminate overload and overwhelm.

Your brain stays directed, busy and happy. You stay focused on what's most important.

ARE YOU KIDDING ME!

The three of us walked up the fairway of the tenth hole of the Legacy Golf Course. Jacob and Rob were players on the men's college national championship golf team.

My role was coaching the team players on the mental and emotional strength-conditioning techniques necessary to stay calm, confident and focused when playing in high-pressure golf tournaments.

Jacob walked over to his ball and prepared to hit up to the green. Rob and I were off to the side, discussing how to keep his mind focused on just one shot at a time.

I noticed that Jacob had stopped and was staring over in my direction. He was not happy.

"What's the problem?" I said sarcastically. I already knew the answer. His look said it all. What he wanted to say was, "Are you kidding me! Shut the *&%$ up!"

But Jacob responded with, "Um, stop talking please."

This was show time for me. Time to see if what Jacob had been taught would hold up on the course. Could he focus under pressure?

I walked over to the middle of the fairway and right up to Jacob. Standing just out of reach of the swing plane of his club I said, "You're going to stand there and tell me you can't focus just because I'm talking. I thought you were a much better golfer than that. You're a champion dude. Are you going to let me get in the way of you getting what you want? Do champions crumble just because the gallery is rude? Do they?"

A big smile of determination came across his face. This was game on for both of us now. He knew what was coming next, and he was ready for me.

We went back and forth in rapid fire. Me asking questions. Jacob answering each one firmly and with conviction.

I started:

> Deborah: *What do you want to do?*
>
> Jacob: *Hit the green.*
>
> Deborah: *Exactly where do you want your ball to land?*
>
> Jacob: *Just off to the right and slightly above the cup.*
>
> Deborah: *How do you need to feel to make that happen?*
>
> Jacob: *Calm, confident. I trust myself and my skills.*
>
> Deborah: *What specifically do you have to do to ensure your success? What's your plan?*
>
> Jacob: *Breathe, E-magine the flight, trust myself, commit, step over the ball and strike the sweet spot. I keep my balance all the way through.*
>
> Deborah: *What's keeping you from making that happen?*
>
> Jacob: *Absolutely nothing!*
>
> Deborah: *Then do it!*

I stood my ground and started jabbering some typical swing thoughts at Jacob. My incessant talking sounded like the thoughts that might go through any golfer's head when they doubt themselves.

Jacob's entire mind and body were ignoring me. He was in his own zone. He went through his pre-shot routine, stepped over the ball and swung through. It was the exact shot he had described.

The smile on his face and the confidence he had just gained were incredible to experience. Jacob had just proven to himself that he could focus his mind on command and perform under pressure, and in the most unusual and disruptive situation.

His acute awareness of what he wanted and the ability to focus his mind and manage his emotions paid off. His confidence shot up and his score went down.

Did you notice how the questions were focused on and specific to the desired results and the execution that was necessary to make those results real?

Jacob knew what to think, how to feel and how to behave to reach the desired results. He created a mental, physical and emotional state of high performance.

BRING YOUR ULTIMATE GAME

When you want to bring your ultimate game, use the 6 "A"s of Acute Awareness. Use this to exercise to bring about specific results from any upcoming meeting, conversation or performance.

Just imagine yourself going into an upcoming business situation. Maybe it's a meeting with a client, a negotiation, a presentation or a sales meeting.

Or imagine you are just about to sit down with one of your kids and have a conversation. Maybe you are looking forward to a performance of a lifetime. Now that you have that image in your mind, go to the next page to create focus, clarity and confidence.

6 "A"s of ACUTE AWARENES

1. Aware

- What specifically and exactly do you want to achieve?

- What is getting in your way?

2. Ask

- What do you need to be thinking to achieve successful results?

- How do you need to behave to be at your best?

- What do you need to believe about the other person, the circumstances, the situation or yourself ... to be successful?

3. A.C.T.

- Access your E-magination to see, feel and believe the successful results.

- Choose the emotion that applies to your specific situation. Do you need to feel confidence, clarity, dominance, power, calm or relaxed? You choose.

    – Take action—it's time to execute. You know what to do and how to do it . . . now do it!

4. Assess

    – This is really important and is often missed. Take the time that is necessary to look at what just happened due to your actions. Assess what went right and what you would do differently the next time.

    – Consider: How will you think, behave and feel differently the next time to get upgraded results? What adjustment can be made to your plan to improve the outcome?

5. Adjust

    – Make any adjustments to you or your plan, so you can improve your results and increase your success ratio.

6. Appreciate

Appreciation is huge for creating consistent success routines.

This is one of the most important and most overlooked aspects of success.

Appreciation is not soft or weak; it's science. Humans need to engage emotionally in our experiences of success. When we do, our ability to remember and repeat that success pattern goes way up.

Athletes show appreciation by patting each other on the butt or doing a dance in the end zone. My golfers are taught to have a "party in their head." They celebrate a great shot with internal excitement and maybe a fist pump. Then it's back to calm, clear and confident.

Think about this. Leaders praise employees, but who praises the leaders? Learn to praise yourself.

Bottom line—you are responsible for you. Learn to give yourself specific, exact praise and appreciation for a job well done. It's imperative to continuous and consistent success.

Repeat this exercise anytime and anyplace. You will gain greater clarity and greater confidence. Imagine how much more successful you will be when you plan for success and achieve it during any parent–teacher conference, relationship, business meeting, parent–child communication, sports competition, and on and on.

CHAPTER TWELVE

SELF-Identity

When YOU matter to YOU . . .
what others think of you won't matter.
— **Deborah Dubree**

Let's get personal. Why should anybody want to work with, take advice from, or buy from YOU? What's so special about you? What have you done lately that matters—really matters? How are you different from your competition? What's your edge? Your differentiator?

This is not about personality types or discovering your values. I've never found that to be particularly helpful.

People standing around the office sharing their personality types is a way to provide excuses for their behaviors: "Oh, THAT's why I cower in a corner at networking events." "THAT's why I boss people around." "THAT's why I never get anything done."

Knowing my personality type never changed my behaviors or my actions. I just end up with a bunch of different and cute labels to call myself. Interesting, maybe. Not helpful.

GUTTURAL and GUTSY

I learned to bet on me. Who I am and who I know I can be.

Having my individual and personal "SELF-identity" has sustained and strengthened me during some of the roughest times in my life.

I originally came up with my SELF-identity when I was sitting on the floor in my living room, agonizing over whether to submit my résumé for the construction accounting position.

Armed with a legal tablet and pencil, I began to write the answer to the questions, "Why me? Why would anyone in their right mind hire me for a position I'm not qualified to do?"

Over an hour went by. Dozens of crumpled-up pieces of paper were thrown all over the living room floor. I felt ticked off, pissed off, frustrated, angry, sad and exhausted. I couldn't come up with an acceptable or reasonable answer.

After walking into the kitchen, splashing cold water on my face and jumping up and down to get the circulation back in my legs, I sat back down on the living room floor.

Then it hit me. I had been looking at this all wrong. The question I needed to answer was, "Why NOT me!"

My past flooded back into my memory. I was that person who in a year and a half graduated high school, graduated cosmetology school, took my state board exams in Chicago, landed my first W-2 job as a hairdresser, married my long-time boyfriend, quit my job as a hairdresser and started my own one-chair beauty shop in my home, and gave birth to my daughter. All accomplished a month before my nineteenth birthday.

I started to think, "Holy crap! Anyone would be lucky to have me!" This was way different than how I had felt just fifteen minutes earlier.

The answers to the question, "Why NOT me?" came gushing out. The words were descriptive, empowering and filled with confidence and courage. They were the real me. Guttural and gutsy!

> *I am gutsy, tenacious, intelligent, ambitious, curious, street-smart, extremely well organized, courageous, determined, dedicated and eager to learn. I put what I've learned in to action, ask a lot of smart questions, expect answers and will do what it takes to be successful.*

I would not have found this in any personality test or values list. This was me in my own words. This description of me, when I say it out loud or to myself, gives me the power and clarity to carry on.

"I"DENTITY IS KEY TO EXCELLENCE

You cannot outperform your "I"dentity. This is how you think about yourself when you are all alone with your thoughts.

Strong people can often will themselves through a performance. But then they are faced with their feelings of doubt, concern, worry, fear and being overwhelmed when they are all alone. It happens to the best of us.

The question is not if it will happen. It will. The bigger question is what to do when those feelings and thoughts hit like a ton of bricks.

What we are talking about is timing. How long are you willing to stay stuck in the downward spiral of negative and self-deprecating thoughts and emotions? They will eat you up if you let them.

NO WIGGLE ROOM

A strong SELF-identity statement is one of the best ways to stay motivated and leverage your strengths. Your SELF-identity is the foundation for every decision you make and action you take.

Remember your statement. Repeat it, feel it and act like THAT person. Think like that person would think. Believe what that person would believe. You are that person. There is no wiggle room. This is you!

Grow up and stand up. Get clear on what makes you special, unique and driven to achieve. Always bet on you. Once clear on who you are, at the very core of you, use the statement anytime you are challenged.

OUTSMART THE CHALLENGES

Whether you are just starting out or you've been in business for twenty years, this simple and extremely powerful exercise of discovering your SELF-identity will give you the courage and confidence you need to take action on what you keep thinking about … but have not acted on or achieved.

When you are clear about who you are, it becomes both your backbone and the backbone for every decision you make. You can more easily say "yes" to what matters and "no" to what doesn't matter.

You outsmart any challenge that threatens you. Throughout my career, I used my statement repeatedly and in different situations.

In the beginning, I said it every morning to gain courage. I continue to use it every time I feel afraid or begin to drop back into average. When I doubt my abilities or myself, I say my statement with deep conviction. I feel the words, "I am tenacious, gutsy, street-smart, intelligent, ambitious, curious and courageous!"

My entire body shifts. I quickly follow up that statement with questions to myself. "So now what? What the hell are you going to do about it? Get off your ass and prove it!! What actions are you going to take right to show that's who you truly are?"

The questions and the challenge to yourself will pull you into action. Remember, your mind loves to answer questions. Give it the right questions and it will give you answers that will propel you forward into action.

Here is what I know: Knowledge and education are important. But people who know who they are and will do what it takes to be successful will surpass the educated average people every time.

I know it because I did it. By the time I reached management level, every meeting I sat in or conducted was full of people who were more educated than I was.

Let me correct that. They had been in school longer, earned a degree and could tell you what to do "by the book."

I had guts, grit and a more practical education. I learned through experience. Lots and lots of experiences. I knew things that were not ever going to be found in any schoolbook.

Because of my background and self-knowledge, I was the one who excelled past the others. I knew who I was and what I wanted for myself. Plus, the best teacher anyone could hope for had taught me. My dad.

He was my greatest teacher. Earning his GED when I was in seventh grade, he was the smartest man I have ever met.

He taught me how to think logically, thoroughly and carefully. I learned how to problem-solve and how to ask a lot of questions.

Curiosity and investigation was a way of thinking and acting. I learned about the cycle of life and death, as well as the cycle of a car engine. He taught me how to not just look at things. We examined them, explored them and figured out why and how they worked.

During visits to my grandparents' farm, my dad taught me the value of working hard and seeing the results of that hard work. To have pride in producing desired results. To push hard and never give up or give in.

The work ethic of my business peers was good. They worked hard and long hours. But I had learned to focus my attention on what would bring me the greatest results the fastest. I still worked hard and long hours, but I got shit done!

Thanks Dad!

Your SELF-identity will keep you focused and in action. Remember, execution is key. This exercise is equally powerful for entrepreneurs, executives, parents, children, athletes and any other person who wants to stop struggling and start excelling.

Business professionals use their SELF-identity statement to bolster their courage before walking into a critical meeting or important presentation.

Football players use it on the sidelines to stay focused and powered up during the intense pressure of a game.

Children use their statement to remain calm and feel courageous when visiting the dentist, on test day, or starting a new school year.

Golfers I train have told me they write a three or four word version of theirs on their golf glove. As they look down the shaft of their club at their ball, their statement is a reminder of who is holding the club. Who is about to make the perfect swing.

Strengthen and empower yourself by writing your own SELF-identity statement.

WHO ARE YOU, REALLY?

Get guttural and gutsy when you answer these questions:

1. Why you? What makes you so special? List some of your characteristics? Think back to when you were a kid. What do others appreciate about you? Remember compliments you have received.

2. Describe what it's like when you are at your very best, high performing self. Write anything that comes to mind.

3. Review what you have written. Now choose the words that really resonate with who you are and who you know you can become. Just let it flow.

Test Your Statement. Say one word at a time and notice how it makes you feel. Some clients grade the power of each word on a scale of 1-10. Then choose the most powerful.

Write your SELF-identity Statement. Carry it with you. Post it where you will see it often. Fully embody it.

NOW – BE THAT PERSON!!

CHAPTER THIRTEEN

Talk and Walk

Win–Win Combination

Master your talk and walk, so you can impact and influence perceptions! Perceptions others have of you, your talent and your abilities. Also the perception you have of yourself.

How you talk includes your internal self-talk and how you talk to others. Your walk includes body language. The non-verbal conversation you have with others. Also the internal power and conversation you can gain by how you move your body.

Being the only woman in a room full of men was unsettling at the beginning of my career. Keep in mind this was in the early 1980s and this was the construction industry. I felt uncomfortable and the men in the room often felt as uncomfortable as I did.

Plus, I was very aware that the men were all more business savvy then I was. And they knew a whole lot more about construction than I did.

Being respected and accepted was my goal. I hate looking or feeling stupid. Losing at this was not an acceptable option.

I looked for any kind of leverage I could find. Learning how to impact and influence through verbal and non-verbal communication became an extremely powerful combination that helped bolster my success ratio. It was something I could manage and work to master.

When I was a Chief Financial Officer (CFO), it was my responsibility to meet with and negotiate with the corporation's CPA, attorney, insurance brokers and banker.

My high school diploma didn't match up well with their multiple degrees of higher learning. But I had leverage. I had me!

When meeting each one for the first time, I set the guidelines and tone for our future relationship. The initial meeting was always in the conference room at the company where I worked. This gave me the home field advantage.

Prior to the arrival of the expert, I would go into the conference room and set my tablet and pen at the head of the table. This reserved my seat and gave me the power position.

When the receptionist would tell me that the expert had arrived, I would walk into the conference room with my head high, shoulders back and a smile on my face, and I would extend a firm handshake. My walk was a little brisk, showing I was a person with things to do.

My tone was always friendly, powerful, comfortable and professional. A tiny, sweet voice was not the impression I was going for.

Eye contact was critical. So was building rapport. I helped them feel more at ease quickly, so we could get to work.

After a few polite "get to know you" exchanges, I had my little saying that went something like this: "Let's just Dick-and-Jane our conversations." *(For those of you who are too young to know the term Dick and Jane, it refers to a "Fun with Dick and Jane" series of children's books from way back in the day. The phrase meant, let's keep things really simple.)*

I would continue, "You can impress me with all of your fancy jargon and I can impress you with construction terms. Then we will both walk out of here not understanding what the other one said. I'd rather get right to the point and not dance around each other. Let's keep things simple and precise. Does that work for you?"

Their whole demeanor would change. All the pretenses would drop. We could help each other look good and help both of our companies prosper. Win–Win–Win.

IMPACT AND INFLUENCE

Knowing how to walk into a room with power, poise and dignity will set the tone for a personal or professional meeting. Then it's time to build rapport and manage the outcome. Not control it. You can't control how others think or behave. But you can manage you, the tone and the outcome. Here are some ways to do that.

Start by matching and mirroring how the other person sits or stands. If they cross their arms, cross your arms. If they frown, frown back at them. Don't mimic them. I'm talking about subtle movements.

Subtle movements like leaning into the conversation when he or she is saying something you are interested in hearing. Then, just for fun, lean back and away from the other person. Notice his or her facial expression and conversation change.

You can even match the tempo of their speech to build rapport. Or you can deliberately speak faster to create urgency or slower to calm things down. Each method changes the tempo of a conversation or meeting.

Simply lowering you voice or raising it will change up the tone of a conversation. Shifting your breathing pattern will too.

When a conversation is getting heated, begin to breathe more slowly. Your clarity and confidence will remain strong. You have the upper hand.

All of these techniques can be very helpful for negotiations, playing poker, and building very positive relationships.

Want to have some fun? Try going into a meeting with someone, and once he or she begins to speak, you stop talking. Watch how you can influence and impact the other person's conversation through doing nothing at all.

GIVE UP DANCING

How you say something is just as important as what you say. People often dance around what they want to say.

Ask someone where he or she would like to go eat and you'll hear, "I don't want fast food. I don't want to get dressed up. I don't want any place that is too noisy."

Oh, my gosh. Could you just spit it out! Where DO you want to go? Stop being vague. Stop the dance. Stop the madness.

And then, there is the tone of voice. If someone is talking in a whisper, how can he or she be taken seriously? Where is the conviction about what he or she is saying?

Tempo can also work for or against you. Notice, what is your natural speech rhythm when you feel most powerful? When you're nervous, that rhythm changes. It's your job to notice and bring your tempo back to a your natural rhythm.

You can do this by changing your breathing pattern. A very simple yet effective technique is through tapping your natural rhythm out with your fingers. Tap the side of your leg, your arm or even a table top. Notice your breathing, heart rate and speech pattern as they fall in rhythm with your tapping.

A DAY OF OBSERVANCE

1. Pick a day to observe how you talk to others.

2. Observe, don't judge, what you say and how you say it.

3. Listen for your tone of voice and be aware of your tempo.

4. Then, decide how you can upgrade future interactions. What, specifically, will you do differently?

POSITIVE THINKING IS USELESS

When I ask prospective clients what techniques they currently use to ensure consistent high-level performance, they proudly state, "I'm a real positive person!"

My question to them is always, "Then why are you calling me?" Their silence says it all.

My next question is, "How well does your positive thinking work for you when you're under stress?" The universal response? "Not so good."

Positive thinking works really well … when someone already feels positive. It can reinforce and motivate lots of joy and happiness. Goodie, goodie!

If someone sits on a mountaintop and hums all day, then positive thinking can be very useful. How often do you get to do that? I'm guessing your day is full of stressful situations, decisions and actions. Positive thinking is useless under stress.

STOP TALKING TO ME!

Have you ever been pushed and pressed to meet a deadline? You scramble to beat the clock and know people are depending on you to produce.

How helpful is it to repeat over and over again, "I am wonderful. I am talented. Everything will be just fine!"

It's not useful at all! If anything, the levels of frustration and anger shoot up and clear thinking becomes impossible. Raging, ranting thoughts and emotions take over. You want to yell at your mind, "Stop talking to me!"

IT'S A PACKAGE DEAL

The mind, body and emotions are a package deal. They work as a unit. Change one of them and the others adjust accordingly.

If your thoughts are on a rampage, get up and move around. The physiological change will help you upgrade your thoughts and the corresponding emotions.

You can't have happy thoughts and sad emotions at the same time. Or vice versa. It's impossible.

It is your responsibility to stay aware of what you are thinking, feeling and the actions you are taking. Awareness comes first. Own Your Talk and Your Walk!

DOWN & DIRTY
WITH DEBORAH

For the past few years, I have had the honor of being a member of the Kwamie Lassiter's Sports Talk radio show. My segment on the show, and the name of my blog, is Down and Dirty with Deborah. So, I decided that is was appropriate to have a section in this book called Down & Dirty with Deborah.

Kwamie Lassiter spent many years in the National Football League with the Arizona Cardinals, San Diego Chargers and St. Louis Rams. In 1998, he led the NFL with eight interceptions. In 2001, Kwamie tied the NFL record of four interceptions in a single game, against the Chargers. He was named Walter Payton NFL Man Of The Year in 2002. I am proud to call Kwamie my friend.

Buckle up! This section will go fast. I'll be sharing a few more proven success insights and strategies. Pay close attention to how you can act on these strategies and insights for your own professional and personal benefit.

CHAPTER FOURTEEN

Insights and Strategies

PERMISSION TO COMPETE

A creative man is motivated by the desire to achieve, not by the desire to beat others.
– Ayn Rand

I'm a competitor. I like to win. There are no bonus points for holding back. Achieving success is a great motivator for achieving more success.

Competing against the best brings out the best. It is frustrating to watch people who are unwilling to really compete full-out. Some act like winning is a sin. Others quit right before they have the chance to win.

Competition is what makes us great. We are meant to compete. Anyone who tries to stifle his or her own competitive spirit is creating a sin. Stop waiting to get ahead.

Find creative ways to compete. Some of my best competitions have been me-against-me, setting my standards high and then busting my butt to surpass them.

You don't need permission to compete. You don't even need a competitor. Your job is not to out-perform the person next to you. You have zero control over what they do. Instead, out-perform your own stats!

Compete with yourself to get better, quicker, more efficient and more effective at what you already do. Find new and different approaches to achieve more. Then, raise the bar and do it again.

THINKING IS OVERRATED

There is a time and a place for thinking. I like thinking. But too much thinking can be both harmful and hurtful to any performance.

Use thinking when you are strategically planning a performance, a golf shot or a power play in business. Think when you are developing, strategizing, practicing and training.

Then, let go of thinking. Do what you do best. Act with intuition and instinct. Playing your best should be just that . . . playing. If you are thinking about your best game, you are screwed. Just play.

Golfers are known for overthinking every aspect of their golf swing. It even has a name—swing thoughts. They worry about the shot they missed or the one they might mess up. And then they overthink the shot they are about to take.

When golfers commit to a shot, step over the ball, trust they know exactly what to do and how to do it, their intuition takes over. They explode through their swing and their game improves.

Think to plan. Think to learn. When practicing, think and adjust as you go through the process. When it's game time, commit and trust. Let go of thinking and just do what you do, the way you do it best.

This is just as true in the boardroom, locker room, on stage or in a sales presentation. Trust yourself, your knowledge and your skill.

THEY LIKE ME; THEY REALLY LIKE ME!

Sitting around the conference table, my vice presidents and I were in a discussion about leadership. I asked each of them to write down the top ten qualities of a good leader.

Each of them had "being liked" at the top of their list. It was tenth on mine. That was a problem.

At the beginning of my career, I would have listed "liked" at the top of my list, too. I really wanted to be liked and to fit in. I felt it was necessary for my success. Plus, it felt good to be liked. I quickly changed my mind.

Being liked is a bonus, not a necessity. People can like a person who is in a leadership role, but not trust them to make good solid business decisions. They can like that person and not fully respect them or their leadership abilities.

When all hell is breaking loose, people will follow who they trust and respect, not who they like. You want to be the "go to" person. The one people count on to perform under pressure. The one fully equipped to take command of a crisis.

Be the one who has the skill set to make decisive choices and take bold action. Respect is earned by being fair and consistent each and every time a decision is made.

- List the ten qualities that you believe a good leader should possess.

- What number would "liked" have been on your list before you read this section? What number would "respect" have been?

- Look at your top three. What are you willing to do to excel in those areas?
- How specifically will you act differently in the future?

FIND A DIFFERENT ANGLE

See if you can relate to this. After I reached the status of owner I began conducting leadership trainings. Every Friday morning at 6:00 AM, the vice presidents and managers would gather in the conference room.

On this particular morning, I made sure I was in the room first. Taking my seat at the head of the conference table, I waited. All the guys started arriving. Laughing and telling stories, each took his seat.

Their butts barely hit the chairs when I started giving orders. "You, go get me some rubber bands. You, I need a legal pad. You, grab a stapler and get back here fast!" They all started to get up from their chairs, looking at each other sheepishly, searching for some additional direction or comfort. In their confused state, I barked, "Go! Get it and get back here!"

As each one came back into the room, smiling with the satisfaction of a job well done, they handed me their "prize" and took their regular seat.

Then I said, "What are you doing? Go sit where your stuff is!" In their absence, I had moved all of their belongings to different places at the table.

After a quick look around the table for their stuff, they began to get up and move to a different seat. Their discomfort and uncertainty of having to sit in a different seat was painfully obvious.

I got up and changed my seat, too. It felt strange. The view from a new seat was weird. It offered a whole new perspective. It was uncomfortable. Breaking a habit always is.

We are all creatures of habit. That one silly, but powerful, game got us all thinking. During our discussion, we each identified how we could change our perspective. How we could begin to see things in a different way, within the company and the various departments.

At our next weekly meeting, I arrived to see one of my managers sitting in what was typically my seat at the table. It felt strange and different, and yet I loved it. He was taking initiative and being decisive. He was changing the rules of who sits where. On a grander scale, he helped change how we could view ourselves and each other differently.

– What about you? Are you stuck in any old habits? Could your views of some people, places, situations, relationships and events use some upgrades?

– What has been holding you back from ultimate success? What if you were to take a different perspective, could you figure out a new plan of action?

– What will you do within your company, career and life to see things differently?

MY CONFESSION

I shocked my vice presidents and managers with my opening statement at a weekly leadership-training meeting.

"There are two things you need to know about me: I am lazy and I am selfish." I meant it.

Early in my career, when I was a construction accountant, I realized that I needed to be strategic about how I could accomplish more than my peers. My knowledge was slim, but my desire to both succeed and exceed all expectations was huge.

It was important for my growth that I come up with a way to do more, be more and provide more to those working above me in the food chain. My goal was to impress. To be noticed and to be indispensable. I needed to outsmart the obvious.

Being lazy was not about effort. It was and still is important to put in the hours necessary to get the job done and done right.

My version of laziness was to find every way possible to work smarter. I needed to do more in less time. Not have to think so hard or so often when any task was going to be repeated.

Developing cheat sheets was critical. Every repeatable task and process was tracked, cataloged and filed. All files were color-coordinated, of course. This saved me so much time and it kept my errors to a minimum. Both made me look good to my boss.

> – Where could you buy some more time by having systems, cheat sheets and tracking?

ABOVE and BEYOND: This is where most people in any position stop. This is also where average and ambition meet and separate.

I began to go deeper and wider in how I approached getting noticed and appreciated. I was selfish, meaning I took it upon myself to take care of my Self, my position, my reputation and my career, while still keeping others in mind.

I began to listen intently to critical or strategic points in conversations. Not gossip. That would have been useless, time consuming, and stupid. I'm referring to real conversations that mattered.

Overhearing many of the management-level conversations, I learned about the company, along with the problems that were happening on various projects. Also, I recognized what areas each person in management felt was most important. I learned a lot and I learned it fast.

I combined my observations with my habit of creating cheat sheets. Two really important results came out of this.

ANSWER LADY: First, I quickly became the answer lady. I could put my fingers on facts faster than anyone. When you hold the power of having answers, it's amazing how people flock to you when they need something.

Being the person that others can depend on is important. It should never be taken lightly or misused. I was their trusted source. I knew it and never abused our relationship.

Often, the need for an answer was quick and critical. The person seeking the answer was attempting to keep him or herself out of hot water. They didn't want to feel embarrassed or stupid.

When a project manager, vice president or even the owner came to me, I would joke with them. Get to know them. I would never belittle them for not already knowing the answer. Why would I ever cause them pain? It was at a time when they were vulnerable.

I cared about them and the company. I gave them what they needed most. I never asked for anything in return. This created a bond of mutual respect and trust.

Having the answers that others sought was really more about me. Now they knew my name. I was no longer just a number.

- What are you currently doing to ensure you are not just a number? Is it working? What else might you do?

SMARTER THAN YOU THINK: Secondly, I appeared to be much smarter than I really was at the time. I simply had systems. Systems for capturing important knowledge on cheat sheets.

What started out as a method for my own fast-track learning, quickly became a way to provide sought-after information. Later it grew into me being included in discussions about projects or ideas that were being kicked around by management team members.

Then they began to ask for my advice. This was a huge turning point. It came at a time when I had actually learned enough about the company to give advice.

Plus, I had what many were seeking and lacked. Logical thinking, problem-solving skills, combined with an inquisitive mind. The exact skills that I had learned from my dad came in really handy. And, now I had survived and thrived through many of my own life experiences. This added to my valuable knowledge.

In return, I could safely ask for their advice. Instead of separation because of our positions on the totem pole, we had full-on collaboration. Everybody won! Including the company. We all thrived.

When I decided it was time for me to learn, grow and be seen even more, I asked if I could do a ride-along out to one of the construction sites. There was zero hesitation. I would walk the sites with a project manager or foreman who would proudly teach me the nuances of construction. It was great!

When it came time for a promotion, guess who put in a good word for me? Told my boss I was a team player? Let him know that I was a valuable asset who was liked, respected and could be trusted? Everyone I had built a relationship with happily jumped in!

YOU ARE ACCOUNTABLE TO YOU: Jumping back to my weekly leadership trainings with the vice presidents and managers, my lazy ways of not wanting to think any more than necessary followed me throughout my career.

I created simple systems to track what each member of my team committed to accomplishing. If they stated they would achieve it, I tracked it in their individual file. Of course, the files were color-coordinated by person.

When any one of my upper management team walked into my office for any reason, I pulled his or her file. I answered their questions. We strategized over solutions. They updated me on what they had or had not achieved.

Then we would go one step further. I would look at their file. They were held accountable to their own words. We could quickly review their commitments versus their accomplishments.

- Do you have a reliable system to ensure your managers, staff, assistants or virtual assistants are held accountable to their own commitments?

HOME AGAIN, HOME AGAIN: An extra little ditty for you. I used this same philosophy and cheat sheet system at home.

As a single mom with two wonderful, active and growing children, I needed to strategize and organize at home, too. Plus, ensure I was teaching my kids accountability.

Groceries became a big deal at our house. We all liked to eat. But I hated the pleading I went through each week to simply come up with a grocery list.

"What do you want this week? How many of that do you want? Do you also want X? PLEASE get the list done! I'm getting groceries tomorrow on my way home from work."

So of course, I developed a system. I created an Excel spreadsheet. I included every food item, cleaning product, dog food, snacks, toilet paper and shampoo that any of us typically needed or wanted on a weekly basis. I also left some blank spaces for the newly added or one-time-only items.

Then, I put all of the items on the spreadsheet - wait for it - in columns. Each column represented the appropriate grocery store aisle where the item could be quickly and easily found.

My kids would simply highlight the items they wanted. Then they would write the number next to the item to indicate how many of that item they wanted. Easy, right?

The list was on the refrigerator all week. Plus, twenty-four hours prior to grocery day, I would make the announcement, "Mark what you want, I'm going to the store tomorrow!"

For the most part, they got exactly what they wanted. If they didn't, they got exactly what they marked. Any complaints or whining about not getting their favorite ramen noodles or mac and cheese were met with a copy of the list. *"You don't mark it, you don't get it."* Simple!

It made for a vastly improved memory, along with the awareness that you are responsible to you, for getting what you want. A lesson many adults have not yet learned!

JOB DESCRIPTIONS ARE ONLY GUIDELINES

I have always found that job descriptions are too restrictive and constrictive for people with ambition, talent, intelligence and creativity. They are a good guideline, but people need to be able to color outside of the "job description" lines.

I like results-based thinking. Agree on the results. Agree on the schedule and timeline. Agree on a budget, if applicable. Agree on the quality that is expected. Agree that there are certain lines that cannot be crossed, without further discussion. These are usually based on either legal or financial liability. And then, let the person prove him or herself.

When the agreed-upon results are met in all areas, trust goes up for everyone involved. Bigger and better projects can be tackled in the future.

Always assess, adjust and discuss what went extremely well and what will be improved upon next time. And reward the individual financially and with appreciation. Creativity and ambition are a rare combination. Individuals win. The company wins. The clients win as well, when job descriptions are guidelines and not handcuffs to improvement.

SECTION FIVE

THE 7 "C"S OF EXCELLENCE

CHAPTER FIFTEEN

What It All Comes Down To

It takes guts to be great.
It takes exceptional courage to reach excellence.
– Deborah Dubree

HERE'S WHAT IT ALL COMES DOWN TO

You have read the book, and by now, you have learned that:

- Average is an addiction. Accepting average is accepting failure.

- Average thinking leads to average behavior, which leads to average results, which leads to average and sometimes catastrophic consequences. You pay the ultimate price for remaining average.

- You have a choice to stay average or pursue excellence. One of the most important aspects of choosing excellence is execution. You must take action.

- When people attempt to fit in, they fail. Always bet on you. Know who you are and what you want. Develop a plan, focus on execution of the play, while keeping an eye on the results.

- Don't believe your own BS. Pick and choose your emotions. Use the 6 "A"s of Acute Awareness for ultimate success. Develop your SELF-identity to remain strong, focused and courageous under any circumstances. Engage your talk and walk for greater impact and influence.

There is much more, but by now, you either get the importance of moving out of average into excellence or you don't. Mediocre stays mediocre.

Top performers build a competitive edge. They go after what they want. They pursue excellence. They push the boundaries and they push their performance. They expect to succeed. It all comes down to The 7 "C"s of Excellence.

THE 7 "C"S OF EXCELLENCE

**Choice. Consciousness. Change. Courage.
Confidence. Commitment. Consistency.**

– CHOICE

First you must make a choice. Remember every choice has consequences. Make a bad choice, and you deal with the consequences. Sometimes catastrophic consequences. Make the right choice, and you enjoy the consequences. Choose wisely.

Only you can decide what the right choice is for you. Not your family, friends, fans, society, media or the person on the street corner. YOU decide.

Freedom comes with making your own choices, no matter what anyone else says. What will you do when you are at the edge of your hopes and dreams being fulfilled and everyone is screaming don't do it? This is the point of choice.

It's your choice. Remember, you are the product of the *'yes's* and *no's'* that you make throughout your life. Choose wisely.

Choices are moment to moment. Even the smallest of choices can create massive change. The choice to turn in my unqualified résumé for the construction accountant position changed the entire trajectory of my personal life and my professional career. I chose to bet on me and at the same time I made a choice not to bet on what society would have believed was reasonable or possible for a girl with my background and education.

Really get this. With every choice, there is an opposing choice. If you choose to turn left, you cannot also turn right. If you choose to be disciplined, you cannot choose to be sloppy.

When you make a choice to pursue excellence, you also make a choice not to stay stuck in average. Choose wisely.

– CONSCIOUSNESS

Consciousness is a choice. Sleeping through life is a habit. Stay conscious. Stay awake. Stay aware. Excellence requires your undivided attention.

Average people are only aware of the obvious. They come up with obvious answers and solutions. No one gives a crap.

Excellence is achieved by observing nuances, so you can

outsmart the obvious. This is where the sweet spot exist.

Great musicians and singers create sweetness. They find the nuances between the individual notes that are written on a flat piece of sheet music. When they perform everybody stops, closes their eyes and listens. Everyone wants to drink in the music and fully experience genius in action.

When you choose to be conscious you will impact and influence others. You will be at your ultimate best. Others will want to experience your genius. They will flock to be near you.

It is your responsibility and no one else's, to remain aware of what is most important to you at any given moment. Focus your consciousness on excellence.

– CHANGE

Stop running from change. Change is inevitable. Pursue it and embrace it. Change is necessary for growth and excellence.

I didn't say you would like change. People are naturally much more comfortable doing the same thing over and over again. This is a recipe for mediocrity.

The more you pursue, embrace and conquer change the easier it becomes to navigate through the emotions that surround change. I promise you this is true. You build a new habit of expecting success from change.

Change helps you feel alive. It keeps you interested and interesting. The cycle goes like this. Face a challenge, conquer it, and celebrate your success; and then its time for more change.

Go find the next level of excellence to conquer. The one that scares the crap out of you and excites you at the same time.

Ask and answer the question, "If I can do THAT, what else can I do?" Then go do it. Excellence is only possible through change.

– COURAGE

He who is not courageous enough to take risks will accomplish nothing in life.

– Muhammad Ali

Courage is part of your job description. It is necessary for making bold decisions and taking ballsy action. Courageous people still feel fear. They just don't let fear stop them from getting or doing what they want. They remain focused on results and committed to making those results a reality.

Soldiers and first responders are courageous. Daily, they face life-threatening danger. They know the risk and do it anyway.

When asked, they would not describe themselves as courageous. They will tell you that they are just doing their job. That is not their humility shining through. It's what they believe. It's how they operate.

The NFL players I coach consider getting the crap beat out of them each week is just part of their job. They know the risks of concussions, lost memory, lifelong aches and pains and debilitating injury. Yet they do it anyway. They don't see what they do as courageous. It's their job. They are focused on performing with excellence to get the results they desire. It's what they do.

Courage comes in all sizes, shapes, situations and circumstances.

It also takes courage to make a decision. Not just any decision. This isn't a "flip a quarter and hope for the best" type of decision. I'm talking about the tough decisions. The decisions others are afraid to make. The decisions others will tell you that you shouldn't make. The decisions that could change your life forever and for the better when you take action.

It takes courage to get up on stage or in front of a room full of people when you're scared to death to speak in public.

It takes courage for a small child to step onto a bus for the first time, their little lip quivering, eyes watering up and tiny little hand nervously waving good-bye.

It takes courage for their mommy or daddy to watch the bus pull away when what they really want to do is go grab their child, hold them close and tell them everything will be okay.

It takes courage to speak your truth knowing that others will disagree.

Courage is necessary to reach the rest of The 7 "C"s of Excellence. Making a choice, remaining conscious and following through on change are acts of courage. Confidence is a reflection of courage. Commitment and consistency would not be possible during difficult times unless you are courageous.

When you pursue excellence, you must be prepared to make courageous decisions, and take courageous actions consistently. Stay focused on performing at your ultimate best and achieving the results you desire. Courage will begin to come naturally. It's part of your job description. It's what you do!

– CONFIDENCE

Confidence grows in proportion to the courageous decisions you make and the courageous actions you take. Success grows confidence.

Even if you screw up, figure out what went right and what went wrong. Stop doing the things that screwed up the results and do more of what went right. Your confidence will grow.

You will begin to take bigger and bolder risks because you stop beating yourself up when things don't turn out the way you hoped or expected. Instead you assess, adjust and act again.

Remember, excellence is a pursuit. Confidence doesn't grow with perfection. When done right, confidence grows through courageous decisions and courageous actions, no matter the results.

– COMMITMENT

If you say you are going to do something, do it. When and how you said you would. If you say you are not going to do something, don't. Kinda, maybe, almost committing does not work.

Make a commitment to yourself to know what's right for

you. Your commitment is your promise. It is your word. Your word matters.

Make a commitment to do what's best for you. Commit to what you want and stay focused on achieving it.

When it gets hard to keep your promise—and trust me, it will—buckle down and do it anyway. This is where courage becomes imperative. Then re-commit and make it stick.

– CONSISTENCY

Build consistency in the way you think, how you feel, what you believe, in your actions and in how you show up. This is your ultimate Self. You trust yourself. Others will trust you. They know you are reliable and dependable.

Be consistent in your execution toward your desired outcome. Waffling and wavering kills results. Stick with it, even when things don't happen exactly how you planned or when you planned. Remain consistent in your determination and discipline.

When others think that their advice is something you just can't live without, let them know, "I got this!" Their opinion does not matter. Yours does. Consistently push yourself toward excellence!

PUSHED INTO EXCELLENCE

My mom almost screwed up my entire life. Executing The 7 "C"s of Excellence is not always easy.

When I was seven years old, I was playing with my brother at our next-door neighbor's house. Our friends were peeking through their screen door, giggling, while my brother and I would run up the steps on their front porch, jump off the side and then run to the stairs and do it again. Kids being kids. All is fine until somebody gets hurt, right?

That somebody was me. On my third jump, I caught my foot on the rose bush, fell, and broke my right arm. Not a clean break. I pinched a nerve and an artery at the elbow.

Did I mention it was the first day of summer vacation? And that I was right-handed?

A specialist was brought in because of the serious nature of the break. Surgery was intense. I had twenty-two stitches, plus nails placed on both sides of my elbow to pin it in place while it healed. Repairs were made to minimize the damage to the nerves and artery. There was a lot of crying (Mostly me, but also my mom. Dad silently shed a few, too).

Side note: here is another "C"—crying. Sometimes crying comes with great enthusiasm, great sadness, concern, disappointment or amazing accomplishment. There may not be crying in baseball, but sometimes there is in excellence.

On a routine office visit, just prior to when the cast was going to be removed, the doctor told my mom she needed to begin teaching me how to use my left arm and hand. He stated that I would be left-handed permanently. He explained that I would never have full use of my right arm or hand. The damage had been far too severe. He was direct, stern and certain. That's how experts are.

My mom was stunned at first. She was at the point of **CHOICE**. My little eyes became fixed on her. Mom stood up, straightened her skirt, and reached down to gently take my good hand.

With tears rolling down both cheeks, she looked at the doctor, and with fire in her eyes and conviction in her voice, she stated, "She was born right-handed and she'll be right-handed." We marched out of the office hand in hand.

Most parents would have accepted the obvious. The doctor is always right. He was the expert. You don't question the experts, the authority figures. Remember, this was back in the days when women didn't speak up.

Imagine it. You must agree with the doctor. What other answer could there possibly be? Don't question, don't think for yourself, and certainly don't make a bold statement that is completely unreasonable or impossible. How crazy is that? Mom, what were you thinking?

Mom made a **CONSCIOUS** choice, in that moment and under pressure. She took action. She didn't give a damn what the doctor thought of her or her decision. She took a risk.

Mom was about to **CHANGE** how both she and I thought and acted from that point on. She stepped into her **excellence** with **COURAGE.** She was going to do whatever it took to do what she knew was right for her little girl.

I didn't know what had happened. I didn't realize the magnitude of that moment until many years later. It was a decision that rocked Mom's world and set an example for my future decisions.

All I knew was that for the next eight months, my mom sat with me daily and we exercised my little right arm and hand. She was **CONFIDENT** that she would make this work. She would get the results. We could do this together.

The pain was excruciating for both of us. I endured the physical pain, while Mom had to endure the emotional pain of hearing her little girl crying out, "Please, mommy, can we stop now? It hurts so bad!" Yet we continued.

Her **COMMITMENT** and **CONSISTENCY** paid off. I have full use of both my right arm and my right hand. The doctor was wrong. His thinking was limited, and so were his solutions.

Even in her fear, Mom had the courage it took for her excellence to shine. How different my life would have been if she had made the obvious choice. Instead, she demonstrated to her little girl exactly what it takes to be courageous and expect excellence.

Thanks, Mom!!

MY 7 "C"s of EXCELLENCE

Repeatedly I am asked, "How does a receptionist with a high school diploma become CEO of a $20 million construction company?" I'll tell you how I did it.

I did just what my mom did. I followed The 7 "C"s of Excellence. Except, I started with a **Bonus C—CHALLENGE.**

Everything begins and ends with a challenge. I **CHALLENGED** myself to be more, do more, have more than what was reasonable or possible for just a small-town girl with a high school diploma. I challenged myself to "not accept average."

At every level of growth, I made a **CHOICE.** I chose to push myself again and again in my pursuit of excellence. I made a choice to follow through and keep getting more of what I wanted.

I remained **CONSCIOUS.** Conscious of the results I wanted and the results I was achieving. I was conscious of where and when

I screwed up, so I could adjust and go again. Also, I remained aware of opportunities that were beyond the obvious. The ones that, when achieved, would have huge payoffs.

CHANGE came fast and furious throughout my career and life. The good and the bad. The struggles, grief, pain and agony were unbearable at times. The joy, happiness, deep satisfaction and pleasure kept the rollercoaster of change always in my favor. I learned that change is good and often great fun. Every time I took a risk and made a change, I felt more alive. I was excited and knew I wanted even more.

My **COURAGE** grew every time I took action. I learned that I could mess up and get up. Each and every time I did, I gained greater courage to take bigger and bolder actions.

CONFIDENCE in my Self, my abilities and my decisions grew right along with my courage. I took immense leaps of faith that even had me wondering how I did it. But I did. I learned to own my confidence. There were times when everything in my body screamed, "Don't do it!" But I did it anyway. I was confident that things would always work out. I would make them work out.

My **COMMITMENT** was to my kids and to me. I was committed to do what it took to get what I wanted. Believe me, it was hard, lonely, scary and painful at times. But it was worth it. When I wavered, I would re-commit and go again. I knew that we would always come out on top. It was my job to ensure that happened.

CONSISTENCY in the way I thought, felt, believed and acted was a key factor in my success. My consistent faith and trust pulled me through and up.

I bet on me, relied on me and depended on me. Whatever else

or whoever else came and went, I was the constant factor I could always count on.

By staying focused on what mattered most, the amount of successes far outweighed what didn't work out. Consistency wins!

Everything begins and ends with a **CHALLENGE!** Once I became really good at something, learned to master it, then it was time for a new **challenge!** Time to raise the bar. Time to begin the cycle up to the next level of excellence again. Excitement and excellence were about to play together again!

BONUS "C"
THE CHALLENGE

You made a choice to pick up this book and read it. You chose to consider me an expert and to read what I had to say.

Will you choose to be average? Will you? You can put this book down, go about your life and consider this a good read.

Or you can take the challenge, break the addiction to average and move into excellence. I can't put in the effort or do the work for you. I wouldn't even if I could. What will you do next?

MY CHALLENGE TO YOU!

1. Make a choice. What is one thing, just one thing, that you can go and do right now that will move you closer to excellence?

   - Think about your career, performance, relationships, finances, or any other area that comes to mind as a priority.

   - Don't think too hard or too long about this. Big or small, do just one thing to get you moving into excellence.

2. Take action. Go do that one thing. Do it now. Go!!

3. Notice how you feel. Recognize what it is like to take action on just one thing. Notice how it raises your confidence. Motivates you and excites you to do more, be more and have more.

Now, go back through the steps and do it again and again and again.

Build your new habit of success and excellence.

You got this!

CONGRATULATIONS!!

BE CONNECTED

INTERESTED IN HIRING DEBORAH ...

- Keynote, Workshops, Seminars, Trainings
- One-on-One Coaching and Consulting
- VIP Day

Contact Deborah at: info@DeborahDubree.com

ClearEdge Office: 480.585.0420

COACHING and CONSULTING DELIVERED ...

By: Phone / SKYPE / In Person

FREE GIFT

Visit DeborahDubree.com to receive your gift of a downloadable version of The 7 "C"s of Excellence

DIRECT CONNECT ...

Down & Dirty Blog   DeborahDubree.com/Blog

Website: DeborahDubree.com

Contact us: info@DeborahDubree.com

ClearEdge Office: 480.585.0420

SOCIAL MEDIA ...

Facebook: DeborahDubreeFanPage

Twitter: @Deborah_Dubree

Linked in: Deborah Dubree

ABOUT the AUTHOR

With only a high school diploma, Deborah went from answering phones as a receptionist to owner and CEO of a $20 million commercial construction company.

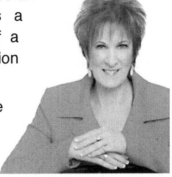

During her climb up the corporate ladder she gained a unique perspective on business and how to beat the odds, outsmart the obvious and reach ultimate success.

DEBORAH DUBREE

She is not average.

From the locker room to the board room, Deborah's clients appreciate her NO BS attitude and real-world application. Clients include business professionals, entrepreneurs, sales professionals, managers and their teams. Also, college and professional golfers and football players that include NFL players from:

- Baltimore Ravens
- Green Bay Packers
- Dallas Cowboys
- San Francisco 49ers
- San Diego Chargers
- Houston Texans
- Tennessee Titans
- Cleveland Browns

Her ClearEDGE™ methods incorporate over thirty-seven years of study, application and implementation of the most advanced positive psychology, neuroscience, brain research NLP, hypnosis and scientifically proven cutting-edge stress reduction technology.

On the personal side, Deborah is a proud single mom of two amazing children. Both her daughter and son are happily married and live nearby. Of course there are the four-legged family members. Deborah's golden doodle, a grand-dog and two grand-cats.

As an adventurer and risk-taker, Deborah has enjoyed cage diving with great white sharks; snorkeling the Great Barrier Reef in Australia; driving a 600 HP NASCAR-style racecar averaging over 124 mph; hot air ballooning over the migrations in Kenya, East Africa; exploring New Zealand; and photographing cheetahs taking down prey in Tanzania, East Africa.